Finding a Mentor Being a Mentor

DONNA OTTO

HARVEST HOUSE PUBLISHERS
Eugene, Oregon 97402

Cover design by Left Coast Design, Portland, Oregon

FINDING A MENTOR, BEING A MENTOR
(Compiled from *Between Women of God* and *The Gentle Art of Mentoring.*)
Copyright © 2001 Harvest House Publishers
Eugene, OR 97402

Library of Congress Cataloging-in-Publication Data
Otto, Donna.
　　Finding a mentor, being a mentor / Donna Otto.
　　　　p. cm.
　　ISBN: 0-7369-0642-8
　　　　1. Christian women—Religious life. 2. Mentoring in church work. 3. Church work
　　　　with women. I. Title.
　　BV4527.O89 2001
　　253'.082—dc21　　　　　　　　　　　　　　　　　　　　　　　2001024679

06 07 /BC-BG/ 10 9 8 7 6 5

In tribute to
my Aunt Pat, Patricia Sayad—
an encourager to one frail girl

Dedicated to
Elisabeth Elliot Gren—
an encourager to millions
and
The Mentors of Scottsdale Bible Church

Acknowledgments

The following people assisted in this book. There would be no book without them. I am forever grateful.

Anissa Otto

Betty Fletcher

Dr. Darryl DelHousaye

Scottsdale Bible Church

Mentors for Mothers Staff

The daughters of my heart

In my many years of involvement with mentoring, anyone could get tired of hearing about the process, yet David, my husband, never expressed frustration with me, the topic, or the time it takes. God truly meant for this man to be my husband.

Contents

From My Heart to Yours

1. The Classroom of the Heart 11
   Answering the Call to Become a Mentor

2. Is It Time for Me? 21
   Stepping Forward into a Titus 2 Ministry

3. The Value of Vulnerability 31
   Taking the Risk to Develop a Relationship

4. Between Women of God 43
   *Welcoming a Younger Woman into
   Your Heart*

5. Daughters of the Heart 59
   Growing Deeper with God Together

6. Caught in Comparisons 67
   Accepting God's Plan for Who We Are

7. A Unique Way of Giving.................... 81
   *Being a Titus 2 Woman to Your
   Friends' Daughters*

8. Frustrations and Farewells 95
   *Facing the Challenges of the Mentoring
   Relationship*

9. Rave Reviews 105
   *Celebrating the Blessings of the Titus 2
   Ministry*

10. The Fingerprint of God.........................113
   Continuing to Be Touched by God's
   Transforming Power

11. Our Privilege 123
   Titus 2 in Action

Tools for Developing Successful Mentoring Relationships

A Touch of Grace: 131
   A Visit with Elisabeth Elliot Gren

30-Week Mentoring Guide
   1. *The Character of a Christian* 142
   2. *Taming the Tongue.*.......................145
   3. *Reasons to Stay Home* 149
   4. *Disciplines of a Godly Womam* 153
   5. *Fashioning Your Mental Wardrobe*..........156
   6. *Being Imitators* 159
   7. *Unity* 161
   8. *Knowing and Finding His Purpose.*.........164
   9. *Busyness* 168
   10. *Trying Trust.*...........................172
   11. *"At-One-Ment"*..........................175
   12. *Serving.*................................178
   13. *How to Love Your Husband* 181
   14. *The Way to Your Husband's Heart* 184
   15. *Building Your Mate in Love* 187
   16. *Communicating with Your Mate.*...........190
   17. *How to Simply Submit* 193
   18. *Intimacy.*................................195
   19. *Diagnosing Your Children.*................198
   20. *Training the Will of Your Children* 201
   21. *Disciplining Your Children.*................204
   22. *Praying for Your Children.*................208

23. The Ministry of Motherhood 214
24. Learning to Love Your Children 217
25. The Ministry of Your Mansion 220
26. Being the Keeper of Your Home 222
27. Food, Menus, and Hospitality 225
28. Finances and Budgets 229
29. Feathering Your Nest 232
30. Creating Family Memories 235

Mentors for Mothers 239

Supplemental Reading List 247

From My Heart to Yours

My house may be empty, but my heart is not. The subject of this book, the relationships between older women and younger women, continues to fill me. Daily, where once I packed lunches, washed diapers, and made certain the house was tidy and dinner was on the table each evening, I now look for ways to invest in the lives of younger women whom God sends to me.

Titus 2:4 declares, "Then they [the older women] can train the younger women to love their husbands and children, to be self-controlled and pure, to be busy at home, to be kind, and to be subject to their husbands, so that no one will malign the word of God" (NIV). After many fulfilling years as a young wife and mother, I now find myself at that stage in life when I qualify as one of those "older women" called to train (or mentor) the younger women. If you too are at that place, rejoice! It is a privilege—and an exciting one, at that—to be able to train and mentor a younger woman.

Since you have picked up this book, I assume you are interested in developing a more meaningful relationship with other women of God. What better way to do it than to give away what you have received in your own journey as a woman of God? If that is your desire, I say thank you. Thank you for caring about connecting with and mentoring others. May the Father bless you for your desire and commitment.

The passion I have for this approach to serving God and others is significant, and I am certain far too deep to thoroughly communicate. But I want to encourage, implore, affirm, motivate, and excite you to look at what God has planned for you and the next generation. There is a younger woman for you.

Replace the sense of loneliness that comes with the later seasons of life; find a deep abiding sense of satisfaction as you pass your perspectives to starving young women just starting out on the path you are nearly completing. Recapture the memories of the past by retelling them to women who are more than interested. Give it away now—all you know, all you've gained, all you've lost, all the pain you experienced, all the joys you've known, all the love you have for our Lord and Savior. Give it away now, before it's too late.

Don't miss seeing the glistening eyes of hurting young women. Don't miss the eager ears of women needing to know you survived, and not only survived but have joy in your heart. Share with them your acceptance of each age and stage of life as a gift from God. Help them know the source to seek. Acknowledge the disappointments and broken dreams that will never be replaced.

These are what will make the next generation strong, faithful, determined, persevering. The young women in my world, daughters of my heart, have changed me, rearranged me, and brought a quality of life that I never dreamed possible. They are the Energizer battery of life.

If you are a younger woman, take heart—God will provide you with an older woman to guide you in His ways. While much of the material in this book is written to the older woman, you can still glean much about finding someone to mentor you and getting all that you can out of the mentoring relationship. I think you'll also enjoy reading through the 30-week approach for mentoring in the back of the book.

May this task, this journey, be twice as much fun for you as it has been for me.

Looking up,
Donna Otto
Scottsdale, Arizona

*One generation shall praise
thy works to another,
and shall declare
thy mighty acts.*

—PSALM 145:4

1

The Classroom of the Heart

Answering the Call to Become a Mentor

❧

ow many times have you heard yourself say, "If only I'd known then what I know now?" You may have been thinking of something as simple as a foolproof way to stay dry when changing a baby's diaper, or as important as how to balance a career and marriage. Somewhere along the line, nearly every woman wishes she had another woman—perhaps an older and more experienced woman—to help her negotiate the twists and turns of life.

But we live in an age where we no longer have the strong generational ties that we used to have. Grown children live hundreds of miles away from parents. Older parents are put in rest homes. We are losing our heritage, and we women are especially sensing that loss. With nowhere else to turn, we learn to dry flowers by reading magazine articles while Martha Stewart teaches us how to roast a chicken on national TV.

Life used to be different.

Woman to Woman

I grew up in cold, blustery Chicago, where we looked forward to being on the other side of that long midwestern winter. It always seemed like an eternity since we had first seen the ice build up and the city slow down because of slippery roads. Ready to welcome warmth, light, and activity back to our world, we hoped for spring when the city could get moving again. But when spring finally did arrive, our rush to get going was often stalled by too many potholes in the road—potholes we usually didn't see until our front tires fell into them! It would have been nice to have someone point them out before we got stuck.

Life has its potholes, too. But God has a way of using these cracks in the road and the unexpected lessons they can teach. Throughout my life I've been touched by women who have shown me where these potholes were or, if I already had my two front tires firmly entrenched as I sometimes did, who have told me how to get out. The lessons of life they have passed on are practical and encouraging. They are the subject matter for relationships between older and younger women—for what I think of as the classroom of the heart.

Only a few generations ago, lessons were taught in that classroom as women worked together cooking, canning, sewing, and raising children. Today we women are far removed from doing chores together. Instead we press a button to open our garage door when we leave and close it right behind us when we return. We fill our days with what seem to be good, worthwhile, and important activities, and some of them undoubtedly are just that. But we're often losing out on the better, the best, the eternal activities. We're too busy for people and for relationships characterized by intimacy and accountability. We lead fragmented lives, isolated from one another and often estranged from ourselves.

It used to be that when a baby was born, grandmothers, aunts, sisters, and neighbors all showed up to help the new mother learn to care for the baby. Women influenced one another in every area of their lives. They provided help when it was needed, hope when it was needed. In today's more mobile society, young women no longer have the support of neighbors or an extended family. In fact, the State of New Jersey has gone so far as to try to mandate that new mothers stay in the hospital longer than 24 hours after giving birth. Why? So that these women can learn about breast-feeding and caring for their newborns—lessons that were once passed on from generation to generation, from woman to woman. Now people are proposing a law so that we can learn what was once shared so naturally and easily between generations!

The busyness of our culture keeps us from passing on spiritual principles and truths as well as day-to-day lessons. And as the success of William J. Bennett's *Book of Virtues* demonstrates, people sense the loss deeply. Spiritual and moral values are virtually absent throughout our culture. The wealth of spiritual knowledge and down-to-earth wisdom to be learned from women who have walked through the experiences of life is being lost at a time when, more than ever, young women need someone to come alongside them.

My Aunt Pat

Early on I was the recipient of the kind of hands-on caring that women of God can provide. My Aunt Pat is a hero to me and, although she died more than 30 years ago, she taught me so many things that often in the course of my day I think, "Aunt Pat taught me that!" But actually I *caught* these things from her. She lived the lessons I learned best from her.

And she captured one of these lessons in a phrase that has stuck with me all my life. Even when I was a young girl, Aunt Pat could see that I often tackled projects that were way over my head, things I could not possibly accomplish for any of a variety of reasons. That's when Aunt Pat would say, "Donna, do what you can do. Donna, are you listening? Do what you can do."

The first time I heard her say that I was trying to put a zipper (a side zipper, for you seamstresses) into a wool jumper that had a cotton lining which was too heavy for the wool. There I was, a novice seamstress working on my first sewing project. I should have been hemming a skirt, but I was charging ahead with a zipper. "Donna, do what you can do," I heard her say. She was teaching me not to get ahead of myself and end up frustrated. Instead, I needed to do what I could at the time and be content even as I grew in my skills. It was a simple statement, but it has made a lasting impact.

Thanks to Aunt Pat, the list of what I can do is far greater than it would have been without her. She taught me how to crochet, knit, embroider, cook, and make a house a home. She was also a constant model of encouragement to me. Aunt Pat had been ill most of her adult life. She experienced 13 miscarriages, heart trouble, diabetes, and all the complications these illnesses can bring. She spent months of every year in the hospital for one reason or another and died at age 42, yet I never think of her as ill.

Never demanding or self-consumed, Aunt Pat was known for her bright smile and happy heart. Every nurse on the hospital floor looked forward to having Pat Sayad on her rounds. Aunt Pat wore her love of Christ on her hospital gown.

One wise person has observed that "nothing is easier than fault-finding; no talent, no self-denial, no brains, no character are required to set up in the grumbling business."

Well, Aunt Pat had character, and she shared it with me. She helped me become a woman who sought God, and I am grateful.

As I look back, I clearly see how God has faithfully provided other older women—messengers, models, mentors—to lead me along, to show me my Lord and Savior, to share the message of His love in flesh-and-blood, hands-on ways, and to help me with the nuts and bolts of everyday living. Woman after woman helped me find Christ and thereby discover rest and hope, peace and encouragement, health and fulfillment in all that God has for me. Each one delivered her message differently, and each one was effective.

Giving Women

A description of the special type of woman that so impacted my life is nestled in the book of Titus. In this letter, Paul is telling his younger friend Titus, his partner in ministry and student in the Lord, about the kind of relationship women in God's family are to have with one another. Read what he says:

> *Older women likewise are to be reverent in their behavior, not malicious gossips, nor enslaved to much wine, teaching what is good, that they may encourage the young women to love their husbands, to love their children, to be sensible, pure, workers at home, kind, being subject to their own husbands, that the word of God may not be dishonored* (Titus 2:3-5).

Now the lifestyle Paul describes for "older women" is in sharp contrast to the lifestyle of the women in Crete, where Titus was ministering (and, you may note, to the lifestyle of many women today!). But we'll get to that in a minute. In Crete, older women who had raised their children and were now enjoying a measure of free time customarily gathered in the afternoon to sip wine and gossip. (Is that the A.D. 65 equivalent of our going to the mall, working out, or "finding ourselves"?)

In this letter Paul reminds Titus that Christian women should be doing far different things as they grow older in their faith and as they learn to manage life more effectively. In the more mature years it is time for them to "teach what is good" and encourage younger women to "love their husbands, to love their children, to be sensible, pure, workers at home, kind, being subject to their own husbands." And how was this teaching to be done? Not through sermons. The older woman—whose devotion to God was evident in the way she lived—would show by her very example that the Lord demands that His people be self-disciplined, temperate, chaste, respectful, clean-minded, patient, charitable, cheerful, and reverent in their behavior. An older woman who has learned when to speak and when not to and who knows what behavior reflects a genuine heart for the Lord would be a living and breathing sermon!

A Contagious Spirit

This passing on of the knowledge of God, this teaching about how to live a life that pleases Him, occurs most effectively, as in the case of my Aunt Pat, through modeling. After all, it is only natural for young people to learn from what they see. It is therefore imperative that those who are older model what is good (Titus 2:3). The godliness of older women—then and now—is far more important than any personal accomplishments the world might note. What younger women need is not someone with an impressive resumé but a true, vibrant, contagious spirituality. And this kind of spirituality is best communicated not through a sermon or a book, or even through many sermons or an entire library. Instead, this kind of spirituality is best learned when younger women see it lived out right in front of them by an older woman. It must be "caught," not taught, and that means a one-on-one, personal relationship over time.

The Concept of Mentoring

The term "mentor" comes from Homer's epic poem the *Odyssey*. When King Odysseus leaves to fight in the Trojan War, he charges his trusted friend Mentor with the care of his son Telemachus and the management of the home. Mentor trained Telemachus in all the ways a father would train a son, and today we use his name to refer to a trusted counselor, guide, tutor, or coach.

In our culture, the term "mentor" tends to be associated with a specific area of knowledge. Mentors in business help new employees learn the ropes. Mentors in a special Washington, D.C., program help high-risk teens complete high school. In trade unions, a person serves an apprenticeship before becoming a licensed tradesman, able then to work without supervision. My mentor when it comes to conquering the technological world of computers (the battle continues!) is 15 years my junior, but he knows his stuff and is sharing that knowledge with me. Such one-on-one attention, such personal education, is a very effective way to communicate information—as Pastor Bob Shank of South Coast Community Church in Irvine, California, realizes.

Pastor Shank defines "mentoring" as "a deliberate transfer of wisdom from one person to another."[1] He explains that mentoring is purposeful, intentional, and planned; mentoring is a transfer of wisdom based on one's life experiences rather than the transfer of knowledge systems or behavioral techniques; and mentoring happens in a one-on-one personal relationship through time. Mentoring calls

1. Bob Shank in the *Pastor's Updated Listening Guide*, February 1993, vol. 36 (Pasadena, CA: Fuller Evangelistic Association, 1993), based on tape 2660.

for the commitment, focus, and single-mindedness of a person willing to pour his or her life, faith, and knowledge of God into another person.

Like Pastor Shank, Dr. Howard G. Hendricks sees mentoring as "a ministry of multiplication" and "a biblically legitimate strategy for our generation."[2] When we ask ourselves the question (and all of us should), "What am I doing today that will guarantee my impact for Jesus Christ in the next generation?" being able to say that you are mentoring a younger Christian sister is an answer that will stand the test of time. *Mentoring*. It is indeed a biblical concept, though not a biblical word. We see it in the relationship of Priscilla and Aquila to Apollos, Barnabas to Paul, Paul to Titus, Elizabeth to Mary, and Naomi to Ruth.

Paul realized that older women—growing-in-Christ women who have lived longer and experienced more of life—have much to offer younger women. He recognized that these wise women can and should play a key role in passing on to younger women how to live out God's truth in the day-to-day world of being a wife, mother, homemaker, career woman, and someone whose life pleases and glorifies God.

God values the older woman and challenges her to share her wealth of experience and the wisdom and perspective she has gained from that experience. To be growing older is not to be outdated, antiquated, or obsolete. It is being able to speak about God—His faithfulness, His redemptive powers, His willingness to provide for His children, the wisdom He offers for child-rearing, the principles He sets forth for homemaking, the ideals and guidelines He has for marriage and living—because we've walked with Him in the valleys, the meadows, and the mountains of life.

And yes, I switched pronouns on you. The "older women" Paul talks about are you and me! They aren't other

---

2. Howard G. Hendricks in *Seven Promises of a Promise Keeper* (Colorado Springs: Focus on the Family Publishers, 1994), pp. 47, 48.

people—people stuck in the first century or people farther along in years than wherever you and I are. These directives are intended for you and me.

You may be 80 and have much to offer a 40-year-old. Or you may be 20 and find a 15-year-old looking up to you. In either situation, Titus 2:3-5 is a clarion call to women today—to older women to model; to younger women to learn. Your Creator Lord, your Almighty God, your heavenly Father, calls you in no uncertain terms to pass on to younger women your passion for Him and your commitment to His ways. How can you say no?

Things to Think About

- In an average week, how much time do you spend with other women? Where do you see them? What do you do when you're together? What do you especially enjoy about friendships and contact with other women?

- In a sentence or two, state your reaction to God's commands to you in Titus 2:3-5.

- Do you have an "Aunt Pat"? If so, how have you been blessed by her? If not, what would you have appreciated receiving from such an older woman?

- Are you an "Aunt Pat" to someone? Are you giving her what your "Aunt Pat" gave you or what you would have wanted an "Aunt Pat" to give you? More importantly, are you giving her what God would have you give and what she needs?

2

Is It Time for Me?

Stepping Forward into a Titus 2 Ministry

~

*P*erhaps you have a desire to become involved in a one-on-one relationship with another woman of God. However, you may be uncertain about your knowledge, your abilities, or your place in her life. Well, fear not, for I have reassurance, encouragement, and God's loving assurance from His Word.

Fortunately, the woman Paul describes is not necessarily a Bible scholar or an expert or professional in a particular area (although she may be one or the other or both). She has not "arrived" in the areas in which Paul calls her to be an encourager. Her marriage isn't perfect, her parenting is not perfect, her home is not perfect, her witness at the office is not perfect, and her walk with God is not perfect—but she is authentic and growing. She hasn't crossed any finish line or been pronounced "complete." She is simply spiritually older, spiritually more mature. She has been walking with the Lord longer than the women He calls her to encourage.

For this reason, a woman who has a high-school diploma and has never worked outside of her home since getting married 20 years ago has much to offer a young woman with a Ph.D. and several years of experience in the business world. The time we have spent with Christ and the fact that He dwells within us enable us to be a beacon, an encourager, and a guide to those younger than ourselves. Furthermore, we have already found answers to questions they're now asking of God's Son and His Book.

Proverbs 31:10-31 offers a picture of such a woman. The writer begins by asking in verse 10, "An excellent wife, who can find? For her worth is far above jewels." And then the description begins. Although the details of her life (do take time to read them!) may be very different from our world, we can learn much from her example and even from the simple fact that she is described as "excellent."

The words of Proverbs and those we read in Titus are strong words. They may even cause you to have reservations about responding to God's call. And I can think of at least three other common reservations about a Titus 2 ministry that women have expressed to me over the years. Can you relate to any of them?

Older woman—that's not how I want to think about myself! Your feelings are no surprise. There's not much in our culture that commends getting older or values the status that comes with experience. In fact, our culture has a real aversion to aging (we celebrate fortieth birthdays with black crepe paper and rented hearses), we don't honor the aged (and they have so much to offer), and we don't want to admit to getting older (as if it's a secret we can keep!). In my traveling and speaking, I often say, "Will the older women in the audience please stand up?" Ninety percent of the audience may be gray-haired, but only three or four women will stand. This same aversion to aging explains why we dye our hair, have face lifts, and undergo tummy tucks.

A touch of God's grace in my life has been my excitement about getting older. Maybe it's because of the impact of older women in my life, but as I've grown older I have always delighted in the aging process. I couldn't wait until my hair began to be salt-and-pepper gray like Mrs. Schaef-fer, my fifth-grade teacher. Why this passion for aging? As I entered my middle years, the reason became crystal clear to me: I couldn't wait to return to young women what so many older women had given me.

So while most of my peers are doing what they can to hide their wrinkles, sags, poor eyesight, and gray hair, I am reveling in the aging process. I'm 55 and proud of it. I'll never hide my gray! After all, according to Proverbs 16:31, "A gray head is a crown of glory; it is found in the way of righteousness." I want to see those slender, silvery reminders of all God's seen me through, all He's taught me, and all He's given me to share with younger sisters.

Besides, have you ever noticed that there's nothing threatening about a gray-haired woman? In fact, there's something very welcoming about her, with her soft smile, gentle wrinkles, and warm bosom. Yes, as we get older, gravity takes its toll, doesn't it? But a grandmotherly bosom is a welcoming place for a younger woman to lay her head and find comfort, encouragement, and hope. As you think about all this, I hope you're beginning to feel a little bit better about the natural and God-ordained process of aging. We older women have a lot to offer!

∽ *Mentoring Moment* ∽

From the Serengeti Plains in the African country of Tanzania comes a vivid picture of the value of the older to the younger:

> *If a newborn wildebeest does not stand up in the first ten minutes of its life, it will be abandoned. The herd has no choice but to move on, away from all-too-present predators.*
>
> *The elders of the herd—not only the parents—surround the wobbly kneed baby wildebeest, providing warmth and support in an attempt to ensure that it will stand and be ready to move on.*
>
> *Too often we human beings do far less for our younger ones.*

A few years ago, when my peers were talking toning, hair color, and ways to dress so they looked younger, my dear friend and mentor Elisabeth Elliot Gren modeled for me what I always thought was right to do. She did not dye her hair, and she even changed its style to a bun. She practices what she teaches about accepting the gift of aging. She proudly wore her wrinkles and always dressed appropriately for her age. Her example encouraged me. My season was here and I could celebrate—and I still am. I like growing old!

But you may not be celebrating. You may instead share our culture's aversion to aging. If that's the case, ask God to change your perspective on aging from society's warped lack of respect to an appreciation of the rewards and special ministry opportunities that come with our later years. May you come to hear the word older with new ears.

Sounds like a great ministry opportunity, Donna, but I'm busy...and besides, I did the Sunday school teaching/vacation

Bible school/choir/church office volunteering/ committee chairing for years! At the risk of stepping on toes, let me ask you, "What are you busy with—things for today or things for eternity? Things you want to do, or things God wants you to do?" Be honest with yourself. You only get one chance at this business called life, and God will hold you accountable for what you do with that gift. Don't have any regrets! Let me also remind you that none of us ever retires from Christian ministry. Glorifying God, becoming conformed to the image of Christ, growing in the knowledge of our heavenly Father, serving our Lord—these and other aspects of being God's child comprise a lifelong process. So don't be resting on your laurels! And don't be wasting valuable time on things that will be dust and ashes. Be heaven-bound, not earthbound, in the use of your talents, your energy, and your time.

Donna, I have time. I understand the importance of the ministry and the desperate need in today's society. I'd like to be involved, but what do I have to offer? Dear sister, for starters, you clearly have a humble, warm heart and a godly desire to serve and be used by God. That's a wonderful starting point and an ideal position from which to have an effective and life-changing (yours as well as hers) ministry to a younger woman. I know well-educated, high-powered, high-energy young women can be intimidating, but what they don't have in their lives is exactly what you can offer—a reassuring presence, stories of God's faithfulness, reminders that babies don't cry/have colic/wear diapers forever, that God is greater than office politics, and He has a special plan for your life, whatever your marital status. The list of what you can give goes on and on.

Several years ago when I addressed an audience of young women, I asked them, "Why do you want an older woman in your life?" A young woman jumped to her feet and responded, "I need someone to assure me that my three-year-old Jennifer will not be wetting her pants for the rest of her life!" This is certainly something you can give!

The tremendous news is that when God calls, He empowers. And He calls each one of us to this ministry of passing on our love for Him and knowledge of Him, of passing on to younger women how to be godly wives, mothers, homemakers, and women of God in the community, at the workplace, or in the gym. Know that He will provide. He will be with you, blessing you each step of the way as you say to Him, "Here am I. Send me." I know God will richly bless you as you bless the younger women He brings into your life.

God Provides

If you are still hesitating to step forward to a Titus 2 ministry, I encourage you to think about my roses. When I was growing up in Chicago, we lived in a rambling old two-story house built on a small lot typical of that dim, dark, and barren older part of the city. My mother, tutored by the next-door neighbor, worked to add a touch of brightness and color to our home. That was not an easy task in the Midwest where flowers appear for such a short time.

My mother planted two rosebushes just outside the back door. She babied those plants, clipping broken branches, dusting the bushes with powder to keep them dry, covering them in the winter, and keeping them evenly watered. For years and years, those roses in the yard meant hours of work that resulted in maybe 15 blooms (but usually fewer than half that number) each summer.

In the late seventies, when my husband's work moved us to a new home in Arizona and the subject of landscaping surfaced, all these memories surfaced. I never even considered roses. "Roses?" I asked. "Never! Too much work;

not enough reward." But now, 20 years later, I have more than 40 rosebushes in my gardens, each one producing too many blooms to count. In Arizona roses are easy to grow.

I am still amazed by these beautiful blooms. How is it that I, Donna Centanne—an ugly duckling kid born on the wrong side of the tracks to parents of no education, influence, or wealth and growing up in the darkness and dirt of an old part of a large city—am here in the midst of all this beauty?

The answer is simple. I'm here and I'm blessed—by roses and so much more—because of the grace of my sovereign God. He provides. And He alone knows where I would have ended up had He not, in acts of pure grace, provided older women in my life—women who have opened doors of beauty, hospitality, spiritual discovery, creativity, art, apparel, and so much more. "God provides" is the message of my roses to me and, I hope, to you. The Lord uses those roses to remind me of His gracious and faithful provision for me, and He can and will use you—yes, you— in the life of His younger daughters. As He provides for them through you, He will provide for you what you need to minister to them in service to Him.

Blessings on You

As the baby boomers approach their fiftieth birthdays, the number of older women in America will grow. It may be the only time in U.S. history when there will be enough older women to go around. It is my prayer that they will accept God's Titus 2 challenge and freely share with younger women whatever they have learned about knowing God and living a life that pleases Him. It is also my prayer that those of us who have the opportunity right now to be older women to these baby boomers will do so—that we will reach out to them so they will have a model for reaching out to others.

Their message in the future will be the same as your message and mine today because it is God's eternal and unchanging message. But the message we are commanded in Titus 2 to share will be communicated in a variety of ways, each reflecting the unique personality of the messenger. Your relationship with a younger Christian woman—where you find her, how you encourage her, what you do together, the thoughts and feelings you share—will look different from mine and everyone else's. But you can be confident that the ministry you have in her life will be just as valid, just as life-changing, just as important to God's kingdom as anyone else's ministry.

The book of Titus clearly tells us that we women have an important role to play in the lives of younger women, and no one else can take our place. So as you open your life and your heart to a younger woman, trust that God will use you. God may send you to an office so you can influence a younger woman there, or He may ask you to go into your local church and begin a Titus 2 group for yourself and others. He may call you to open up your life to a neighbor, a young woman at church, or the daughter of a friend. No matter what, keep walking with Him and, as Aunt Pat used to tell me, "Do what you can do." As you and I walk with God and spend time with Him, we are changed in the presence of a holy God, and we are able to be all that He desires us to be and to do all that He calls us to do.

Things to Think About

- Do you seek out younger women? Why or why not? If so, what kind of relationships with younger women do you currently enjoy? What kind of relationship with younger women do you most enjoy?

- How do you feel about aging? What thoughts do you have about this inevitable and God-ordained process? What is the root of the majority of your thoughts and feelings, positive or negative?

- List ten things you can offer a younger woman. Let "perspective" start off your list.

3
The Value of Vulnerability
Taking the Risk to Develop a Relationship

~

ave you ever noticed that the first phrase spoken by every angel you meet in the Bible is "Fear not"? The most familiar instance is probably when an angel of the Lord suddenly appeared to the shepherds that first Christmas night. The darkness was broken by the angel's radiance, startling the simple shepherds. That's when the angel said, "Fear not: for, behold, I bring you good tidings of great joy, which shall be to all people. For unto you is born this day in the city of David a Savior, which is Christ the Lord" (Luke 2:10, 11 KJV).

That same message applies when we begin to consider becoming a Titus 2 woman in the life of a younger woman. Stepping out in faith means developing a relationship with someone new, and that means taking a risk. (Opening your heart and your life to an older woman is just as much a risk!) But as we've all been told: Anything worth doing is worth doing well, and anything worth doing will cost something. This two-part bit of wisdom certainly applies to Titus 2 friendships between older women and younger women. The first cost you may encounter as you obey God's command will be overcoming your fear and taking the initial risk of beginning a new relationship.

Facing the Challenge

People deal with fear and new challenges differently. A popular option today is taking a class or going to a retreat or seminar dealing with whatever you're facing. You can enroll in classes to learn how to give birth, care for a newborn, cope with a toddler, encourage children in school, and deal with adolescents. You can take classes on spiritual growth or on learning how to be a witness for Christ in the workplace. The list of potentially useful classes goes on and on.

But when a young woman is struggling with a difficult situation and is certain her situation is unique, she doesn't need a class, a seminar, or a how-to manual. She needs a mature friend, and she will benefit greatly from the presence of an older woman who has walked through more of life and discovered that "this, too, shall pass." She needs a classroom of the heart. The older woman's eyes, filled with compassion, communicate understanding and care; her gentle touch offers comfort; and words learned from her own life experience provide hope and set a standard— God's standard—for the younger woman's life. In fact, the older woman's gracious ways and godly presence may be the most comforting language in the world. And yes, making that connection means taking a risk—but that risk, besides being an act of obedience, has benefits and blessings for both women. Let me give you an example.

The Risk of Imparting Our Lives

"My husband no longer calls me twice a day. He must not love me." When I heard my young friend, newly married, speak these words through tears, I smiled to myself. She felt rejected and unloved and was certain that this change in her husband's behavior signaled a lack of his love. I remembered well those thoughts and feelings.

But I also had a bigger-picture perspective, as any woman married longer than five years would. After all, it never fails that a man's focus changes after he's married. He first conquers his woman and then, to care for her and show how much he loves her, he goes out to conquer his world. And he usually sets aside the behaviors he used to win his wife when he wages the battle to earn a living. Does his change in behavior mean he no longer loves his wife? Certainly not! Yet his new bride often feels pushed aside.

Now, when this young friend of mine picked up the phone and called me, she didn't want me to refer her to a book or a research paper on the subject of men. She didn't even want me to point her to the Bible—at least not yet. Instead, she wanted and needed a person who had experienced the same situation, felt similar pain, and persevered through it. I could do that. I didn't need to know a single resource to offer her. That's not what would help her pass through this storm of fear. All I needed to do was say, "Be not afraid" and offer her some hope. And that's what I did.

But I did so at some risk. Just as she took the risk of sharing her fears, I took the risk of sharing my story and myself. We both took the risk of exposing ourselves to the other.

The apostle Paul knows about this kind of risk. He wrote to the believers in Thessalonica:

> *Having thus a fond affection for you, we were well-pleased to impart to you not only the gospel of God*

but also our own lives, *because you had become very dear to us* (1 Thessalonians 2:8; emphasis added).

In this single sentence, Paul touches on two issues that relate to an older woman/younger woman relationship. First, he uses the phrase "fond affection," something that is fundamental to our role as older women. We must care about the women God sends to us. After all, they are His beloved; they are gifts He offers us to love and encourage, to pray for and teach. We must never regard them as trophies to be added to our display cases or evidence of a prideful obedience to Titus 2. God has entrusted these precious young women to us, and we are privileged and honored to be used by Him and to offer them "fond affection" in His name.

Second, Paul touches on the issue of authenticity and the ability to be real. We are to share not just head knowledge and book learning about life. We older women are to share "our own lives." Only in the bonds of Christian love am I comfortable sharing my weaknesses, my failures, and my ongoing struggles. Christian love means I'll be accepted, not judged; encouraged, not belittled; lifted up, not put down. And that kind of love works both ways in an older woman/younger woman relationship of the heart.

Excellence is willing to be wrong,
Perfection is being right.

Excellence is risk,
Perfection is fear.

Excellence is powerful,
Perfection is anger and frustration.

Excellence is spontaneous,
Perfection is control.

Excellence is accepting,
Perfection is judgment.

Excellence is giving,
Perfection is taking.

Excellence is confident,
Perfection is doubt.

Excellence is flowing,
Perfection is pressure.

Excellence is journey,
Perfection is destination.

So when my friend called, I told her how I cried and cried when David stopped calling me every day at 8:30 A.M. as he had in the years we courted. When I complained to him, his response was so logical. (Of course I did not want logic!) He said, "Why would I call you at 8:30 when you just took me to the train at 6:30?" I don't remember my answer, but I'm certain it was fraught with emotion and confusion.

I've also told younger women who were having problems with envy about the jealousy I felt toward other women in David's life—not because of anything he did or didn't say or do but simply because of my own family history. Sharing our sins, failures, and struggles like this is never easy—not for a younger woman and not for us older women.

An Authentic Life

But sharing our sins, failures, and struggles is the trademark of authenticity. Just as the very real Skin Horse did in its conversation with the new Velveteen Rabbit, talking about what happened to cause our hair to fall out, our eyes to drop out, or our joints to get loose is what authentic people do:

> "Real isn't how you are made," said the Skin Horse. "It's a thing that happens to you. When a child loves you for a long, long time, not just to play with, but REALLY loves you, then you become Real."
> "Does it hurt?" asked the Rabbit.
> "Sometimes," said the Skin Horse, for he was always truthful. "When you are Real you don't mind being hurt."[3]

Living life, being loved, getting hurt, experiencing joys and heartaches, and knowing God in the valley, on the mountaintop, and when He's silent—these things make us real. These things make us authentic. And these things enable us to be to younger women the messengers of God, the beacons of His light, and the channels of His love that they need. Again, we can't teach what we're not. We can only teach who we are. And living a life with the Lord makes us His authentic people, prepared for the ministry He calls us to.

You might imagine how relieved this tearful young friend was to find out that she was not the only wife in the world to be disappointed by her husband; that an older woman she respected had felt unsure in her marriage; that someone else not only had experienced this same situation but had survived it; and that her husband was very normal and probably still loved her very much.

---

3. Margery Williams, *The Velveteen Rabbit* (New York: Holt, Rinehard and Winston, 1983), pp. 4-5.

My young friend shared her own life, and I shared mine. We both exposed some of the fears of our heart. This dear woman found understanding, acceptance, and encouragement simply because I shared a little of myself and my experiences as a wife. Having done so, I could then direct her to the resources I knew about—a videotape on men and how they tick, a book on the differences between men and women, and, as always, God's Word.

First we needed to risk sharing our lives. Then comes the heart-to-heart connection and the comfort that we women of God find when we grow together.

The Risk of Pointing to God's Truth

I'll never forget the time Gloria arrived at my door. She was sobbing uncontrollably. I took her into my arms and just let her cry. Her pain was very deep. Her husband had found another woman, and Gloria was embarrassed, angry, hurt, afraid, and confused. Certain she had made a mistake marrying this man, she wondered how she could tell her parents, and she didn't know what would happen to her now.

After I heard details about secret telephone calls and hidden bills, a letter from the other woman, and the scene of the confrontation, Gloria paused and said, "Donna, I know I am to forgive him—*but!*" What joy I found in being able to simply reaffirm for her that truth in her life. Her heart said, "Run from this pain." Her culture said, "Dump him." But her God said, "Forgive him."

Forgiveness is a process that, unfortunately, doesn't erase the pain quickly. And it is never easy to watch someone we love undergo the kind of heartache Gloria was feeling. But such pain brings us face-to-face with the hope we find only in God. Our heavenly Father is the God of our suffering, not just the God of delightful and happy times. And our

God hurts with us when we hurt. He understands our humanness, He knows our hearts, and He realizes that forgiveness is a struggle for us.

God also knows how important it is for us, His people, to draw alongside one another when our hurts run deep. That is what Gloria needed from me—my presence, my hugs, my tears shed with her. But after we cried together for a while, she needed something else. Remember playing "Pin the Tail on the Donkey"? When it was your turn, a blindfold was placed over your eyes and you were pointed in the wrong direction so that finding the donkey was as difficult as possible. Well, I play a reverse "Pin the Tail on the Donkey" with the younger women God brings into my life. When they come to me I don't blindfold them, and I always point them in the right direction—toward God, His life-giving Word, and occasionally, when they need more help than I feel qualified to give, toward a pastor or more qualified person.

After the storm of emotion faded, Gloria realized that God called her to forgive her husband. At that point, all I did to help Gloria was to assure her of the truth she already knew. I kept her facing in the right direction. Then, during the roller-coaster days and weeks that followed, I continued to remind her of God's truth when circumstances suggested she take a different approach to the situation, and I continued to be available to her. Sometimes her call would come late at night, and then it was often a frantic three-minute conversation that began with, "Donna, tell me again." And I did. I reminded her of God's great love and compassion and of the commands (like "forgive") which He has instituted for our own good.

I also encouraged Gloria to do what she could do just like my Aunt Pat had encouraged me. Gloria could not make her husband turn around and be faithful. She could not change what had happened. But she could continue trying to be the best wife possible. And Gloria did the hard things. She prayed for her husband, she didn't run from the situation, and she didn't kick him out. She loved him and waited, offering him the hope of forgiveness. Each step of the way, just as when she first arrived on my doorstep, she practiced "Be not afraid," willingly risking the possibility of greater pain and further rejection from her husband. She believed that being faithful to God's Word meant letting herself be vulnerable in that way, and I stood by her side with prayer, acceptance, and love.

When a young woman like Gloria faces a difficult situation, feels the deep pain that life can bring, or hungers for an answer, that need—whatever it is—will best be met by someone who has been available to her in the past, someone who has understood her, given her the freedom to be authentic no matter how awful it looked or sounded, and accepted her whatever she was feeling. Getting that close to one another is a risk that both people take, but it's a risk a younger woman willingly takes when she knows a godly older woman will never blindfold her or point her in the wrong direction but will, instead, open her eyes to the love of Jesus and point her to her Maker and His heart of compassion.

The Rewards of Risk

The kind of closeness God grants between women of God is the result of risk-taking. Sometimes the only way an older woman can take that initial risk is by gritting her teeth and acting out of obedience to God's command in Titus, trusting that He will be with her as she does what He says to do.

I know the first step on any journey always seems hardest. You may be unsure of the response you will receive or wonder, "Was that appropriate? Am I doing the right thing?" But read what one woman wrote after taking her initial step: "Today, Tammy and I got together for the first time. I think I'll have to take off my shoes for I'm truly on holy ground. It was wonderful!" God blesses when, in obedience, we step out in faith, trusting Him to be with us.

Being a beacon of God's light and a channel of His love, being Jesus with flesh and bones for a young woman—this can look like an intimidating assignment from the outside. But like any ministry, you'll be covering this special outreach in prayer, asking God to guide you, use you, and bless the time you spend with His younger daughter. He will honor your prayers. Yes, you need to trust that God has brought this young woman into your life in response to your prayers. And yes, you need to trust the young woman as you share with her your own life and heart. But remember that you will never be in it alone. Jesus will always be there with you (see Matthew 28:20). Knowing that the bond of His love exists and that He is there in the relationship with you can indeed help you risk and help you trust.

One more thing. In my Bible-study program Mentors for Mothers (see page 239), the only requirement for mentors is simply that they love Jesus. A heartfelt love for Jesus is more than enough to encourage young women. That genuine love for Jesus also enables us to willingly take a risk for God's beloved young daughters, to extend to them "fond affection," and to be authentic with them at the same time that we allow them to be authentic with us. So be not afraid! Knowing that the Lord is at your side, boldly go out and be a Titus 2 woman to that younger woman God will bring into your life.

Things to Think About

To what current situation or concern in your life does the "fear not" or "be not afraid" speak? If the words seem just words, spend a few minutes in prayer and ask God to help you hear them as His specific message to you.

What do you think of when you hear the word "risk"? What risk have you recently taken? Comment on the outcome and what you learned from that experience. What risk did you recently bypass? Comment on what you learned from that choice.

What about your life and yourself do you find risky to share? What will you look for in a confidante? When you do feel ready to share, pray about your upcoming conversation and then "be not afraid"! Taking the risk of being vulnerable and sharing ourselves builds bridges between us and other people that can't otherwise be built.

4

Between Women of God

Welcoming a Younger Woman into Your Heart

~

*I*f you come to my home for dinner, especially in the winter months, you will probably find a huge apple pie for dessert. It has been a family favorite for about 25 years because it was only then that I mastered pie-baking. (I was a late bloomer in the art.)

I have one of those dandy apple-peeling gadgets that peels and slices at the same time. I found a surefire pie-crust recipe (that's essential). Using a pastry cloth and rolling pin cover help immeasurably. I also settled on those green Granny Smith apples and determined the right amount of butter, flour, sugar, and cinnamon to go with them. Once the bottom crust is in the pan and the apples are in the crust, I create a design on the top crust. Sometimes the design is as simple as the letter representing the person we're celebrating. Sometimes I get a little more elaborate.

But now every pie I make—whatever the occasion—reminds me of an important lesson: "It's never too late to learn something new." And that message is certainly relevant here as you get ready to respond to God's command to become a Titus 2 woman and welcome a younger woman into your world and into your heart.

Of course these daughters of the heart (my favorite description of the young women God has placed in my life to encourage)—daughters in your church, daughters for a season, daughters of the heart whose parenting was weak, difficult daughters of the heart, faltering daughters of the heart, and daughters of your friends—are a wonderfully varied breed, and I've been blessed by a wide spectrum of them. Out of that experience come the following suggestions and how-tos for these God-ordained relationships.

Let me also remind you of the truth of Isaiah 46:4: "Even to your old age, I shall be the same, and even to your graying years I shall bear you!" May the specific suggestions that follow, as well as this promise the Lord makes to you, encourage you in your new adventure and help you truly enjoy the younger woman God sends your way. After all, she is God's gift to you.

Making the Connection

Meeting a young woman may seem like a difficult task, and it may be harder for some of us than for others. But for everyone the first step is prayer. Ask God to bring you a daughter of the heart. Then, having begun to ask God to choreograph a Titus 2 relationship for you, open your eyes and look around. You will probably have to only look around your sphere of influence—the worlds of church, friends, office, neighborhood, volunteer work, kids' activities—to discover God's answer to your prayers. That certainly was the case for us when my husband and I met Kim.

Sent by the Lord

In 1988, David and I met Kim Moeller, and we didn't go out of our way. We met at a church committee meeting. She was lighthearted, bubbly, adorable. Like David, she had been born and raised in Wisconsin. In our casual conversation, we discovered she was single and might be interested in serving on another committee with us. Frankly, one of the main reasons I suggested that she join us was my "Yenta" trait. (You remember matchmaker Yenta in *Fiddler on the Roof...*) You see, there was this dear single man on that same committee...

As our conversation at that evening meeting ended, Kim said, "If I could ever help you in any way, let me know." Never offer to help Donna Otto because I'll always take you up on it!

A month later, I was working on a huge project that kept me from running a few necessary errands. Kim came to mind, so I phoned her. The conversation went like this:

Donna: "Hi, Kim. Remember me?"

Kim: "You bet! How are you?"

Donna: "Fine—and I'm calling to take you up on your offer to run a few errands for me."

Kim (silent for a long time and then finally): "I'd love to, but I don't have a car. I'm riding the bus these days."

Donna: "Well, we have the Old Brown Belle that we offer to anyone in need, and you're welcome to it. Come by and pick it up."

Kim (silent again for an even longer time): "Well, you see, I'm taking the bus because I can't afford to pay my car

insurance. I'm disciplining myself to ride
the bus as a way of getting my finances in
order."

Let me break in here. Kim did not know that David and
I had just been discussing what to do with our home. Since
our daughter had left for college out of state, we had some
empty bedrooms and so had decided to seek the Lord for
someone we could help. Kim couldn't have known about
our conversation or our prayer. Neither could she have
known how much David and I value the kind of openness
and authenticity she had just shown.

Donna (bold as usual): "How much is your car
insurance?"

Kim: "$250 every six months."

Donna: "How much is your rent?"

Kim: "$250 a month."

Donna: "Well, if you came to live with us for 30
days, you would have the money for the
car insurance, and you could help me a
few hours a week in return."

Kim: "Really?"

Donna: "Let me talk to David tonight. We'll pray
and you pray, too. I'll call you in a few
days."

Honestly, our conversation was that brief, that direct
and to the point. David and I discussed the matter. We realized we had only met Kim once, but decided even if she
were Attila the Hun, in 30 days she would be gone!

Seven days later, Kim—with loads of stuff and her little
orange car—moved into our home and into our hearts. She

didn't stay a month; she stayed two years. And during that time, she truly became a daughter of my heart. We worked together, prayed together, laughed together, and had a few spats together.

During her stay, Kim worked with a financial counselor and disciplined her spending habits. When she moved into her own apartment, Kim was not only debt-free, but she had some savings for emergencies as well. We smile when we think about those money lessons and hard-earned bank accounts because when Mr. Right (actually Mr. Robert) came on the scene, he was very careful with a dollar. He might not have been as crazy about a gal in debt!

Two years after Kim moved out of our home and into her apartment, Kim and Robert were married in a lovely morning wedding in our garden. It was picture perfect, if I do say so myself.

> *Simple encouragement can be extremely powerful. For me, one-line gems spoken by two of my own mentors have encouraged me again and again in times of difficulty. The first, of course, is my Aunt Pat's "Do what you can do." The second is Elisabeth Elliot Gren's "Do the next thing."*
>
> *When Elisabeth Elliot's husband, Jim, and his party were speared to death by the Auca Indians in 1956, a stir was created around the world. Leaders from many nations sent words of prayer and comfort to the wives of the slain men and their children who were living in Ecuador. Through this time of pain and questioning, the best advice Elisabeth received from a friend was, "Betty, do the next thing." She looked around and the next thing was not to write a book, or speak a profound word or prayer, or even to comfort someone else; the next thing to do was to change her daughter Valerie's diaper.*

How do you explain this kind of unexpected appearance of a daughter of the heart? Sent by God is all I can say. Of course God sends all of the various kinds of daughters of the heart. He ordains that they be in your life. But there was an extra touch of grace in Kim's arrival. I hadn't initiated the relationship, and I hardly knew her. But I will always be thankful that God had her land on my doorstep.

Sharing Skills and Interests

Here's another example of finding people to mentor right within your own sphere of influence. An excellent seamstress and a godly woman, Carol was taking an advanced class in tailoring when she met Tammy, who was not only interested in being mentored by a woman who knew everything about sewing but who, Carol saw, needed a spiritual guide as well. The two became friends because they shared an interest in sewing, but within a year Carol had introduced Tammy to Jesus Christ, and Tammy had welcomed Him as Lord of her life.

Like Carol, you probably won't have to look far for a younger woman to welcome into your life. Consider the young women God has already put within your reach, those you see regularly, and those you spend time with. Look around your neighborhood, your church, your place of employment, the clubs you belong to, and the classes you take. Chances are the person God has for you is closer than you think.

If you are a young woman, whether you're single or just starting out in married life, or in the midst of mothering and want to be in relationship with an older woman, look for places in your community where older women are involved and make your presence known there. If you feel that God is calling you to get close to a particular older woman, volunteer to serve her as a way to link yourself to her. A young woman in our Family Circles group who asked, "Could I come help you with Poppa?" when David's father became ill and moved in with us has become a dear daughter of my heart. She recognized a need and offered to meet that need, I accepted, and God blessed us with a very special relationship.

But keep in mind that, just as God never forces Himself on us, we aren't to force ourselves on others. Yet know, too, that when we are faithful in prayer about the Titus 2 relationship we desire and take some common-sense steps to get in touch with that older or younger woman we want, God will respond and bring to us the one He has chosen in advance.

For example, I am absolutely certain that wherever you live and whatever church you attend, God has a young woman there waiting for you to pass on to her the godly convictions of your life. In fact, the church where you worship is the best place for you to begin this service to Christ. A house of the Lord is an excellent place to seek a woman with whom to share your lifelong spiritual walk and the lessons you've learned along the way.

Pray for the women around you as you sit in the sanctuary on Sundays. Help in the nursery and pray for the young mothers as they come in, all the while keeping your eyes and heart open for one who needs help. Go to the teacher of a young marrieds Sunday school class and offer to be an older woman to anyone whom the teacher knows needs someone to walk alongside her. Or surprise your pastor and let him or her know that you are available to encourage, advise, or give a younger woman a shoulder to cry on. Don't wait for a younger woman to take the initiative. That's your job—and let me assure you it's a wonderful job to have!

You may be able to be close to more than one young woman at a time, but be careful not to overextend yourself (maybe having a small group of women to lead at one time is your answer). You wouldn't want to miss the blessing that a Titus 2 relationship can be!

Getting to Know One Another: Asking Questions

A lot of women find asking getting-to-know-you questions difficult, and often don't know where to begin. In Mentors for Mothers we've found "A Few of My Favorite Things" a good place to start when an older woman and younger woman first want to get acquainted. If using the following list feels a little awkward to you, begin by acknowledging that to your younger woman and let those words break the ice: "I hope you don't mind my referring to this list, but I really like some of the questions here and thought they would help us get to know each other better—and I really do want to get to know you." If someone said that to me, I'd do whatever she suggested!

What is your favorite...

Color	Song
Breakfast	Type of music
Lunch	Place in the house—and why
Dinner	Piece of furniture—and why
Dessert	Season of the year—and why
Time of day—and why	Holiday—and why
Fabric	Radio station
Way to be touched	Book
Recreational activity	City or town you have lived in
TV show—and why	Childhood memory

Film	Musician
Flower	Gifts you've received
Book of the Bible	Place to study
Verse in the Bible—and	Way to spend money
why	Way to spend time
Speaker—Where did	Favorite anything else you'd
you first hear him/her?	like to share *

Learning to Listen

For years David has kidded me that I am a woman of two verbs: "buy" and "talk." Actually, my tendency to talk too much has been an area that I continue to ask God to change in me. I ask Him to help me listen, and I have to practice keeping quiet. When I am quiet, I find I learn more than when I'm talking. By learning to ask simple questions and then really listening to a younger woman, you will open a path of discovery between you that you will cherish.

The first time I met with Jill Goodman, we sat at a table and shared a wonderfully deep conversation. She was new to the faith and to our church, and I can still remember the moist eyes—hers and mine—as she shared her story. I quietly listened to this woman God had brought into my life through a study I was teaching. The second time we met together, we again sat at a table, but this time we shared a meal. Again, I just listened—and that's not always easy for me to do!

A wise person has said, "Silence is the mother of prayer and the daughter of a holy heart." Take it from someone who knows! Don't talk all the time. Instead, make a conscious effort to really listen to this young woman of God. Hear her words; hear her heart. In doing so, you will be a great comfort to her.

---

* Adapted from Mentors for Mothers

Hearing About Her Goals and Dreams

Once you've broken the ice, don't stop developing your question-asking and listening abilities! A sure way into anyone's heart is to get her talking about her goals and dreams: When you were 12, what did you dream about doing in life? What do you hope to accomplish before you die? What goals did you set for yourself this year?

As author Gil Beers observes, "A question is one of the most wonderful communications devices in the world":

> Reflect back on the last three conversations you have had with someone. Did that person show a genuine interest in how you spend your day, what you like or don't like, what you think about certain matters, and what you would do if you were in a certain situation? I think it's safe to say that you have had very few persons ask you questions like these about your thoughts, your concerns, your convictions, your values, your interests, your reactions, your "heartbeat" about life. Most of us can count these kinds of conversations on the fingers of one hand and have fingers left over.
>
> When I ask you a genuine question about your thoughts...your experiences, or anything else that concerns you, I extend a person-to-person invitation....Remove personhood from heaven or earth and either becomes a sterile test tube devoid of love, grace, truth, peace, friendship, and a hundred other qualities that make life exciting because it is personal.

Not only will asking questions help you get to know your younger woman better, but it will also help your younger woman get to know herself better. Hearing her talk about her goals and dreams will also allow you to pray for specific issues and details in her life. At some point you can ask her about her relationship with the Lord. One of my favorite questions is, "Tell me about your pilgrimage of faith." Be willing to share some of your own story. After all, she needs to get to know you, too.

As your relationship grows, don't be afraid to ask the younger woman how you can help accomplish her goals, especially in those Titus 2 areas of her walk with the Lord, her marriage, her children, and her home.

Offering Encouragement

Encouragement is one of the greatest gifts we older women can give younger women as they struggle to be godly women, wives, mothers, homemakers, and career women in our confused and confusing society. As you get to know a younger woman, you will see some obvious and very personal ways you can encourage her in the challenges she faces and the demands she feels. To help you get started, though, consider the following ten ideas, adapted from a list I've had in my files for years.

- Write an encouraging letter (Paul to Timothy).

- Share how God has dealt with you—your personal testimony of overcoming and growth (Paul's testimony in Acts 22).

- Offer your supportive presence, even when you don't understand (the women at the cross). Don't withhold friendship when a sister stumbles or embarrasses you (Joseph and Mary, Paul and the Corinthians).

- Affirm her worth by showing kindness when she hurts (Jesus in Matthew 25—feed the hungry, visit the prisoners, clothe the naked, and so on).

- Compliment your younger woman on the progress she makes in the faith (1 Peter 1:22; 1 Thessalonians 1).

- Be available and willing to listen (Paul corresponded with the Corinthians when they needed and asked for his help).

- Be a cheerleader—offer celebration when the situation looks dim (Paul and Silas in prison).

- Jump in and help her actually complete a job (John and Peter went to Philip in Samaria, Acts 8).

- Stand up for your sister, defending her when others disparage her (Barnabas for Paul, Acts 9).

- Review with her the record of God's involvement in your past and present, so she can get the future into perspective (Paul to the Philippians).

Sharing Books, Tapes, and Videos

Many fine materials on being a wife, mother, and woman of God are available in Christian bookstores and perhaps even in your church library. Reading a book together, listening to a teaching tape, or watching a video like Elisabeth Elliot's *Peaceful Home* (one I heartily recommend) can be very profitable activities for you and a younger woman. When you choose a video, watch a little of it, stop the tape, and talk about what you've just seen and heard. Take notes as you watch so you can go back and refer specifically to a point that was made. Do the same with audiotapes, and be sure to tackle books in bite-sized pieces, too.

One time I decided to explore a subject area that was entirely new to me, and I invited my daughter of the heart to join me. I simply said, "This is a topic I know nothing about. Do you want to learn with me?" We had a grand time. As we both learned something new, she learned more about me, too.

Setting Boundaries

How often will you meet together? Once a week? Once a month? How long will you meet when you do get together? One hour or two? How frequently will you call one another and how long will you talk when you do? Both of you will benefit when you know what to expect.

After all, if a young woman does not clearly understand who she is in your life and how she fits in, her confusion can interfere with the ministry God has called you to and the blessings He has for both of you. But if you have clearly laid out the parameters of your relationship, your young friend will not be wondering about the rules. She will be able to relax in the relationship, share herself more freely, and receive more completely all that you have to offer her. She will also see in you a healthy example of setting boundaries. At the same time, you will have protected yourself from feeling crowded or taken advantage of. Do you see that having these lines of communication open right from the start will make the relationship work better for both of you?

Taking Time to Review

Open-ended commitments are hard for everyone involved, so let me suggest that right at the start you set a time to evaluate your new relationship. It's usually wise to begin with a limited timeframe: "Shall we meet four times and see where we are?" If you already know this young woman and sense a solid foundation for your relationship, you might say, "Let's plan to meet for six months and then reevaluate." Not having clear guidelines and a specific schedule for when you'll evaluate how it's going can make it hard to end the relationship. Many mentoring relationships will evolve into a "daughter of the heart" relationship, but not all of them will.

But let me also caution you about ending the relationship prematurely. As I look back on my life, I see long periods of time when no growth was evident. So I encourage you to hang on to the woman God sends you through thick and thin as long as you feel it's His will and you sense her sincere desire to learn from you. When you don't see any desire for growth or any efforts to change on the part of the young woman, and when God seems to be giving you permission to move on, it's time to end the relationship. And that can happen more gracefully if, from the start, you've identified points along the way for evaluation.

Such preset points for review provide opportunities to go over the guidelines and boundaries you have established. If you sense your younger friend struggling or wanting more than you are able or feel comfortable giving, clear the air. By doing so, you will keep the relationship open and enable yourself to be used in her life so that she can be all God wants her to be.

Being a part of that kind of growth—being used by God in someone's life to help her be the woman He intends her to be—is truly joy unspeakable. Do you know the old hymn "Joy Unspeakable" (by B.E. Warren)? It says, "It is joy unspeakable and full of glory and the half has never yet been told." Not until we are in the presence of God will we know the full effect we have on the young women God sends our way when we make ourselves available to be used by Him.

Things to Think About

- When you have an opportunity to get to know someone, what interferes with your attempts to make a new friend? What can you do to remove these roadblocks?

- For a less-threatening getting-to-know-you exercise, ask that potential new friend the following questions.

  —What are five of your all-time favorite books?

  —What are two of your favorite movies?

  —What are the topics of two of your favorite sermons?

- What makes listening difficult for you? If listening comes rather easily for you, thank God for that gift. If you want to be a better listener, make that a matter of prayer.

5
Daughters of the Heart
Growing Deeper with God Together

~

If you've ever met around a table for prayer, sharing, and the study of God's Word, you know what God can do when you sit across from someone with your Bible and an open heart and begin to learn together about Him and each other. I haven't done any scientific research, but my experience around a table—the comfortableness, the closeness, the ability to read and write in good light, the chance to look into another person's eyes, the warmth of a shared pot of tea—has taught me that it's an ideal setting for growing deeper with God and your daughter of the heart. I like my dining room table, but any table will work. So once you've gotten acquainted, invite your new friend to your table. Get a cup of something warm to drink, your Bibles, some paper to write on, and a box of tissues, then see what God will do when two women of God come together.

Feeding on God's Word

When my friend's grandson asked for a cookie, she quickly sliced him an apple for a snack, telling him as she did that apples would make him grow up to be big and strong. But even before Grandma finished slicing the apple, three-year-old Brandt had climbed onto the counter and grabbed the cookies. "I don't want to be big and strong," he said as he darted past her, the first cookie nearly devoured. "I want to be fat and widdle."

You and I are a lot like Brandt. We often eat "cookies" and then wonder why we aren't big and strong enough to serve God as we desire. That's why I suggest you spend time studying the Bible with your daughter of the heart. I often turn to the New International Version Serendipity Bibles (call Serendipity House in Littleton, Colorado, at 1-800-525-9563). These Bibles were created for small groups (you and your young woman qualify!). Since they include discussion questions for every passage, they are very helpful tools when it comes to growing "big and strong" in the Lord.

Also look into Bible-study opportunities at your church. If nothing formal is offered, ask for some suggestions about material and do your own study with your younger woman. Christian bookstores offer a wide variety of easy-to-use study guides. Spend a morning with your younger woman looking at material together. If that sounds like more than you want to tackle, look into the Bible studies available at a larger church in your area and attend there. Also find out if Bible Study Fellowship, an international study group, is active in your community. (BSF International's website address is: www.bsfinternational.org.)

Remember, though, that studying God's Word together doesn't have to be tightly structured to be extremely valuable. I know two women, one in her early forties, the other in her late twenties, who met regularly for a one-year period to read and talk about the book of Isaiah. Two others went for weekly drives and memorized a passage of Scripture each week. Just reading Scripture out loud to each other or memorizing verses is a great way to grow together in Christ.

Being Faithful in Prayer

Faithful prayer is a significant element in this God-ordained relationship between a younger woman and an older woman. No one can know the vital role such prayer plays in the older woman's ministry and the younger woman's struggles. In your prayers, ask God to:

- Guide you in praying for your younger woman and increase your concern for her.

- Block the enemy's plans against her.

- Bless her and manifest His goodness in such a way that there can be no doubt that it is His goodness, not coincidence or chance.

- Strengthen every good personality trait and good desire she has, and encourage right decisions.

- Make her open and receptive to His voice and sensitive to her own personal sin and need.

- Release her from any bondage, rid her of any prejudice, and break the hold that sin or an evil habit may have on her.

- Surround her with His holy presence, and remind her of His many past mercies and

His merciful intervention in new and powerful ways.

- Melt away any hesitation she might have
  about moving closer to Him.

- Allow her to know His great and merciful
  love.*

Of course, you will also pray about the specific and
daily concerns your younger woman talks about, but these
listed areas will keep you mindful of her major goals and
such bigger issues as her walk with the Lord, her need for
His protection, and her ability to hear His voice.

Praying Together

"I learn more from people when they are praying than
any other time." These are the words spoken to me by a
dear older woman in my life, and I agree wholeheartedly.
While our prayers are directed to God and for His attention and glorification, the family of God is blessed and
informed as we pray aloud with one another. Your
daughter of the heart will learn about you, your love for
God, your level of authenticity, and most certainly the
depth of your passion for the King.

A few reminders about praying together:

1. *Pray frequently*—on the phone, when you are
   together, and at points in your conversations when appropriate. Let her know that
   you believe God hears and answers the
   prayers of a righteous woman.

2. *Pray honestly.* Begin with confession. Be
   honest before God and her about your shortcomings and failures. Emphasize the fact that

---

* Adapted from Mentors for Mothers.

you believe God cares for all areas of our lives, large and small. This will help point her toward God when she has any need.

3. *Pray in an understandable manner.* Taking your younger woman into consideration, pray in a way that will not confuse or muddle her thinking. Use simple terms and simple phrases.

4. *Pray Scripture.* Do not hesitate to read a passage of Scripture as a prayer, showing her the power of God's Word when recited back to Him.

5. *Pray when you don't have "the" answer.* Make it a habit when asked a question you do not know to stop and ask God for the answer. This pattern will reinforce your dependency on Him for all things.

Make your communication with God time a "Sweet Hour of Prayer," tender and transparent. It is in prayer we receive strength and courage to attend to life as God planned.

Keeping It Simple

Don't become so caught up in going deeper that you forget the life-changing effect that simple moments together can have. Remember, you don't have to be perfect to help your young woman face the challenges of her world. You will do that just by letting her into your life. For a young mother, having the freedom to get away from the kids for an hour may be all she needs to blossom. For a single or career woman, a quiet lunch together may provide the opportunity to refine your younger woman's perspective on life and refresh and encourage her in the challenges she faces.

You don't have to orchestrate deep conversations. Sometimes all a younger woman needs to see is an older woman finding satisfaction in folding a load of clothes. However, if you are working together in the kitchen or folding laundry and a subject comes up about which you would normally stop to pray—by all means, stop to pray! Sometimes you will need to make opportunities, but sometimes you just need to *take* the opportunities the Lord gives you.

Walking with the Lord

Never try to be an "older" woman alone. Instead, let God be part of this ministry each step of the way. Be a woman of prayer and rely on Him to bless you as you minister to His younger daughter. He will be your guide as well as your source of wisdom, patience, and love. Furthermore, through prayer and the Holy Spirit, you have total assurance of access to your daughter of the heart in every situation. I'm finding great comfort in that fact right now as I sense the need to communicate with a dear daughter of my heart. I'm sequestered in a cabin with no telephone so I can finish writing this book, which means I can't speak to her. I can write, but a letter will take days to reach her. Through the power of prayer and the Holy Spirit, I can touch her with God's love today.

May I encourage you to go to the eternal, everlasting fountain of life for a long, deep drink of His strength and sustenance? "Be big and strong, not fat and widdle."

Things to Think About

- What do you most enjoy about your current prayer life? What can you do to improve your prayer life, to increase and/or enhance your communication with your heavenly Father and His Son, your Savior and Lord? What will be your first step toward that improved prayer life? When will you take that step?

- What topic in Scripture would you like to explore more thoroughly? What will be the first three steps you will take toward learning more about this topic? When will you start? Could you and your younger woman learn together?

6
Caught in Comparisons
Accepting God's Plan for Who We Are

~

*M*ixed-up priorities, busyness with the wrong things, inattention to the Scriptures, the absence of prayer and quiet time with the Lord, a lack of fellowship—all these things can interfere with our journey toward Christian maturity (and they do!). But I am convinced by the number of women I have met that one problem stands above the others: the deadly sin of comparison. You know how it goes:

"If only I were as creative as she is..."

"If my husband were as kind to me as hers is to her..."

"If I knew the Bible the way she does..."

"If I had her blonde hair..."

"If I were as thin as she is…"

"If I had her brains…"

We make comparisons like these at all stages of life. Whenever we place ourselves next to other women, we can find an endless number of areas where we see ourselves falling short. Nothing is a bigger source of discouragement, poor self-image, or an ungrateful spirit than this tendency to measure our own worth by what we think we see in others.

The temptation to make comparisons is something you and I need to pay special attention to as we become Titus 2 women. The enemy will definitely use this tendency to establish roadblocks on your journey toward becoming the woman God wants you to be, the woman He wants you to be as you reach out to others. It may also become a source of difficulty if your younger woman begins to compare herself to you. Let's look at some of the ways comparisons can interfere.

Comparison Keeps You from Recognizing the Truth

When my friend or the woman I know only from a distance, if at all, becomes the standard I feel I must measure up to, I am no longer focusing on God's standards for me. I miss His truth. And I miss Jesus Christ Himself, who is the purest standard for each one of us.

Have you ever been to an amusement park with a young child? You head for the roller coaster, ready to pay for two tickets, when you see the colorful sign that reads, "Children must be this tall to ride the Mighty Loop." The smiling clown extends an arm to indicate that magical height, but when your child stands next to that clown, she no longer smiles. Despite her deep breaths and efforts to stretch her neck, she's just too short. She doesn't measure up to a standard which, although based on the size of the roller coaster cars, is somewhat arbitrary. It's not a universal or even meaningful standard, yet it has the potential of demoralizing a "too-short" child. She wants to be as tall as that clown's outstretched arm, but the truth is she's as tall as she needs to be right now. Next summer she'll probably be able to ride the Mighty Loop, but even if she isn't, she is—in God's eyes—exactly as tall as she should be.

When we look to Christ as the standard for who we should be and how we should act, we stand face-to-face with the truth of who God calls us to be. We find hope in the fact that God's transforming power is at work in us to conform us to Christ's image (see Romans 8:29; 2 Corinthians 3:18). We aren't on our own; we aren't doomed to failure. But when we let another woman become our standard for who we think we should be, we find only frustration.

Keep in mind, however, that comparison is different from imitation. God does give us direction about whom to imitate and the importance of taking this privilege seriously. Scripture clearly tells us to imitate those whose lives are pleasing to the Lord:

- Brethren, join in following my example, and observe those who walk according to the pattern you have in us (Philippians 3:17).

- Be imitators of me, just as I also am of Christ (1 Corinthians 11:1).

- You also became imitators of us and of the Lord, having received the word in much tribulation with the joy of the Holy Spirit (1 Thessalonians 1:6).

- For you, brethren, became imitators of the churches of God in Christ Jesus that are in Judea, for you also endured the same sufferings at the hands of your own countrymen, even as they did from the Jews (1 Thessalonians 2:14).

- Therefore be imitators of God, as beloved children; and walk in love, just as Christ also loved you (Ephesians 5:1,2).

As Paul lived for Christ...so I am to watch what he did and do the same things. When we see God's character displayed in the lives of others, we are to imitate it. We are to "be imitators of God."

Someone's Watching You!

We think of him as a painter, but Renaissance master Leonardo da Vinci was a sculptor, architect, and engineer as well. The artist who created the haunting Mona Lisa actually painted only about 15 pictures, and just three of these were women. *Cecilia Galleran* (*The Woman in Ermine*) and the wedding portrait *Genevra de Benci* are the other two, and *Genevra* is a very interesting one indeed because, as was a common practice in his day, Da Vinci used both sides of the wood. On one side, the porcelain-faced beauty captures the viewer's eyes and heart. On the other side are symbols depicting her education, her status in society, and her virtuous character. There is something compelling about the work of art. You can't help but be attracted to this woman. And adding to the intrigue is the conviction of Renaissance scholars that when this painting was first displayed, people did not see Genevra first. Instead, they saw the symbols that represented her qualities. They noticed first her character and then her appearance.

When I heard this fascinating bit of art history, I started thinking about my own life. What do people see when they look at me? What do I want them to see? What trait would I choose for them to notice most? What really matters?

People do watch us. I first learned this one Sunday morning several years ago. A young wife and mother walked up to me when the worship service was over. Her first words were, "You don't know me, but I've been watching you." *Me? What on earth for?* I thought to myself. She continued, "I see how you look so admiringly at your husband during the opening section of our service. And I've noticed your regular attendance, your interest in the sermons, and that big Bible that you carry. Could we have lunch? I'd like to ask you some questions."

During my Sunday afternoon nap later that day, this woman's remarks stirred me. I thought, "What a huge responsibility!" But as I prayed for the young woman and thanked God that I would have a chance to speak of Him to her, I suddenly realized that being with that woman would feel like a job, a "huge responsibility," only if I were concerned about being the kind of person I thought someone should watch. But if I continued to try to be the kind of person God wanted me to be, He would use me in her life however He wanted. If I am truly living for Him, being a Titus 2 older woman is not taking on a different character. It's just being me and letting a younger woman close enough to see who I am and what's inside.

Keep that perspective in mind as you get used to the perhaps new idea that, no matter who you are, where you live, or what you do, someone is probably watching you. What are they seeing? Are you modeling life as Christ would have you live it? Are you putting on biblical thinking each day or is the culture's way of thinking guiding your choices and activities? Are you letting God's Word guide and direct your use of time? Your interactions with others? Someone is watching you. What are you teaching her about God and His kingdom?

Even older women in my life who did not profess Christ often behaved in godly ways. Mrs. Rubel is one example. The Rubels owned a small boutique I worked in when I was in high school. They went out every Saturday night, and made their time together a priority—something that was unheard of in my house.

Just as striking as the fact that the Rubels went out every Saturday was the fact that Mrs. Rubel began getting ready for her date with her husband—fixing her hair, touching up her makeup, changing her shoes and often her outfit—an hour or so before the store closed. It didn't seem necessary to me to "fix up" to go out with the man you'd just spent the day working with, so one day I asked her about her preparations. Her response still echoes in my mind: "Mr. Rubel is the dearest person in the world to me, so I want to look fresh for him across the dinner table."

In so many ways, Mrs. Rubel modeled for me, an impressionable 16-year-old who didn't have any other marriage to watch, how to show a husband you loved him. I was seeing a love-filled marriage, and I was learning.

Although the Rubels' Jewish heritage was different from my Christian faith, I still learned biblical standards during the three years I worked for them. I also saw beauty, culture, respect, wisdom, and consistency—qualities missing in my own life—in their work, their marriage, and their home. Yes, Mrs. Rubel opened her house to me. She lived out the hospitality that we are to show other people,

*and she gave me a front-row seat from which to keep
watching and keep learning.*

Are you modeling a godly woman's love for her husband, love for her children, good sense, purity, effective
home management, kindness, and loving subjection to
your husband? Those are lessons younger women need.

Consider the advice Susanna Wesley's father offered her.
He said that what counts is not to be "rich in money [or, I
would add, knowledge] but rich in character, determination, and intellect." Abraham Lincoln observed, "Character
is like a tree and reputation like its shadow. The shadow is
what we think of it; the tree, the real thing." Character is
real; character is authenticity—and the ability to be
authentic has always been an important goal for me. We
who are commanded to pass on to younger women important lessons about being the people God wants us to be
must be true in our modeling, and that comes with living
life.

Following the will of God—thinking according to His
values, His commands, His purposes, His standards—
enables us to pass on to the next generation our love of and
knowledge of our Lord and Creator. Thinking God's
thoughts enables us to be His beacons, His light, His salt. It
also enables us to watch people, see *their* character, and
learn from them whatever God would show us. And it
enables those who watch us to see God in us and learn
what He would have them learn. This is part of God's plan
and far removed from destructive comparison.

Comparison Keeps You from Being Uniquely You

"For Thou didst form my inward parts; Thou didst
weave me in my mother's womb. I will give thanks to
Thee, for I am fearfully and wonderfully made; wonderful
are Thy works, and my soul knows it very well." These

words of King David in Psalm 139:13,14 (KJV) are words that you, too, can sing—unless you are too busy looking at other people and imagining how you fall short of being like them.

Comparing yourself to other people prevents you from acknowledging the truth that God made you, that He made only one of you, and that He made you unique. Your gifts, your family heritage, your appearance, your brain-power—these characteristics and many others make you totally unique in all the history of the human race. You are an individual, different from any other person, so why do you want to look like, think like, and act like someone else? Why not enjoy the fact that you are a one-of-a-kind and much-loved creation of your heavenly Father?

We can't enjoy our status as God's special children when we insist on scanning the crowd around us to see how we compare. And nothing chips away at our self-confidence like that kind of vigilance. You know how it works. You buy a new dress for a special event. The fabric, the cut, the color, the fit, the price—it's perfect for you and for the occasion. But when you arrive at the party and start looking around and making comparisons, suddenly what was perfect can seem woefully inadequate, can't it? When we do this same sort of comparing of other aspects of ourselves, we find it hard to feel good about being the person God has created us to be. Looking to Him rather than at the people around us can help free us to be ourselves and to enjoy our own decisions, choices, and approach to this gift called life.

Comparison Clouds Our Sense of Who We Are

Author Robert Fulghum tells a story about a game called "Giants and Dwarfs" that speaks to what we can lose when we compare ourselves to others. As a group of children gets ready to play the game, the leader counts them off into two groups. One will be the giants; the other the dwarfs. When the leader finishes, a little girl goes up to him and says, "Where do the mermaids go?" He says, "There are no mermaids"—to which she responds, "Yes, there are! I are one!"

This little girl knows who she is. She doesn't let what the people around her are saying and doing weaken her understanding of herself or undermine her acceptance of herself. Former First Lady Barbara Bush is another wonderful real-life example of this. Clearly, even in the media spotlight, she is comfortable with who she is, and she let her faux pearls and stature become her trademark. It would have been all too easy to compare herself to her predecessor (rail-thin and solid-gold Nancy Reagan), but then Mrs. Bush would have missed out on the opportunity to be who God has made her and called her to be. She would have missed out on the special mission He has for her alone.

So, like the young mermaid and Mrs. Bush, be yourself. Know that you, in your uniqueness, have a niche—a mission and a ministry—that only you can fill. Revel in that special, God-given role and stand strong in the fact that God made only one of you.

Comparison Undermines God's Leadership in Your Life

God has a plan for your life and mine (see Jeremiah 29:11). When we are living out lives as ourselves, focused on Him, we can be sensitive to His leadership as that plan unfolds. We will notice the gentle nudge or firm push that keeps us going in the direction He has chosen for us. But when we compare ourselves to other people and try to act like someone we're not, we may easily miss God's will for our lives. When our eyes are fixed too much on other people, we can't pay attention to the Lord who wants to guide our steps and direct our paths.

Consider the example Jesus gives us. He didn't fit in with the religious establishment of His day, and He didn't try to. Instead, He did what God directed. He didn't use the healing methods of His time. Instead, He offered spittle and dirt, the touch of His hand, His spoken word, and the hem of His robe. He was true to who He was—the unique Son of God, the person God designed Him to be. Because of this, He could respond when God called, and He could do so in the manner God directed. Jesus was Himself, and that freed Him up to be God's perfect servant rather than a slave to peers, tradition, people's expectations, or society's ways.

I haven't always known that kind of freedom. I remember, for instance, when the idea of making goals was first introduced to me. I read over a friend's list of goals and thought, "These look great! I'll do the same!" What a frustrating year followed—a year of almost no spiritual or personal growth. Reading the goals of my friend next to me at that goal-setting seminar made her—rather than my heavenly Master and Lord—the leader of my life for that disastrous year. Always ask yourself, "Whose rules?"

Beware of Your Expectations

We also do ourselves a great disservice when we set unrealistic goals for ourselves and then compare ourselves to that ideal. As we learn to look at Christ's standards for us and to appreciate our own God-given uniqueness, we need to also beware of developing false and unhealthy expectations of ourselves.

To keep from developing such expectations, often we simply need to recognize our limitations. We need to acknowledge the truth about such things as our education, our resources, our family situation, and our physical being. At 5'6", for example, we can't expect a contract with a professional basketball team. If we only speak English, we can't expect an exciting career in international diplomacy. If we have 8 children under the age of 16, we can't expect to maintain a home of solitude. We need to adjust our expectations according to God's leading as well as to the stage of life we are in, the gifts and talents He has blessed us with, and the ministry to which He has called us.

As you begin sharing your life with another woman of God, consider how much you are still laboring under this burden of not living up to expectations you've had for yourself. What have you expected that has not come to pass? Were those unrealistic expectations? Have you failed to acknowledge that the sovereign God created you to be exactly who you are and placed you just where He wants you to be?

Resting in God's sovereignty is key to following in the apostle Paul's footsteps and learning to be content in all circumstances (see Philippians 4:11). It takes practice to learn to accept God's plan. It isn't easy to die to oneself. But when you and I don't accept God's plan for who we are or where we are or what we are doing, we mock His perfect ways and His perfect love. Comparing ourselves to unrealistic expectations for ourselves as well as to the women around us is wasted energy. Such comparisons rob us of being all we can be in our service to God, our families, and our friends.

Now say again with David—speak the words aloud and wholeheartedly—"Thou didst form my inward parts; Thou didst weave me in my mother's womb. I will give thanks to Thee, for I am fearfully and wonderfully made; wonderful are Thy works, and my soul knows it very well." Amen!

Things to Think About

- What comparisons between yourself and other women do you find yourself making most often? Why do you think you are especially sensitive about that/those trait(s)?

- What can you do to change your habit of making comparisons? What does God's Word say to you about your value to Him, your Creator? How can God's Word and His Spirit help you change your pattern of thinking about yourself? What is the first step you will take toward freedom from comparing yourself to others?

- Complete the following statements about yourself. Let this exercise help you appreciate the unique and wonderful creation you are.

I am a...

I wonder...

I hear...

I see...

I want...

I am...

I pretend...

I feel...

I touch...

I worry...

I cry...

I am...

I understand...

I say...

I dream...

I try...

I hope...

I am...

7

A Unique Way of Giving

Being a Titus 2 Woman to Your
Friends' Daughters

~

As you may have already discovered, you have a unique opportunity to be a Titus 2 woman to your own daughter, and you may also play that special role in the lives of your friends' daughters. These two types of special relationships are to be cherished and handled with great care.

Your Own Daughter

One way to cherish and protect your relationship with your daughter is to evaluate your motives as you develop a relationship with another young woman. If you are seeking a young woman to mentor because your own daughter has left home, hurt you, or disappointed you, you are only inviting further grief in your relationship with her. Daughters of the heart must not be a part of your life so that you can show your own daughter what a wonderful woman you are. I've seen this happen. One woman I know, though unaware of what she was doing, flaunted her relationship with her younger woman before her biological daughter. When the situation reached fever pitch, the yelling began and the truth came out. Surprised by what she realized about herself, the woman asked her daughter to forgive her, but the pain lasted for a long time.

My point is this: Your own daughter must never be put aside for a daughter of your heart. In my relationship with Kim, whom we talked about earlier, I have always sought my daughter Anissa's counsel in areas where I was unsure. For instance, Kim lives in our town, but our daughter lives in California. It's easy for me to pick up some extras at the market for Kim, and no one minds that. However, when Kim first moved in, it was imperative that I talk to Anissa about which room would be Kim's. Anissa willingly shared her own bedroom with Kim, but that is an arrangement I certainly never would have made without Anissa's input. Then, on another occasion, I had a Christmas gift idea for Kim, but I felt led to ask Anissa what she thought about our giving Kim a certain item from our home. Anissa responded openly and honestly, saying, "Gee, Mom, I'm not sure. I may want that myself someday." And David and I respected her wishes. We would never push our own daughter aside in the least little way and put another woman ahead of her. (At the same time we mothers are careful with our own daughters, we must also not let them dictate what God would have us do in nurturing a young woman God sends our way.)

The Teacher
Lord, who am I to teach the way
To little children day by day
So prone myself to go astray?

I teach them knowledge, but I know
How faith the flicker and how low
The candle of my knowledge grows.

I teach them power to will and do,
But only now I learn anew
My own great weakness through and through.

I teach them love for all mankind
And all God's creatures, but I find
My love comes lagging far behind.

Lord, if their guide I still must be,
Oh let the little children see
The teacher leaning hard on Thee.

—LESLIE PINCKNEY HILL (© 1921)

When you open your life to a younger woman, you need to remember that your natural daughter is in a very different category from any other woman God calls you to reach out to. Your own daughter needs to know that she is not being usurped, replaced, pushed aside, demoted, or slighted. She needs to know that you love her as much as always and that absolutely no other relationship with anyone else will ever change your love for her.

When your own daughter rests secure in your love for her, the rewards for both of you will be immeasurable. I know I will always remember one of the more tangible rewards I received from Anissa years ago. A tiny little package came in the mail. The accompanying note read, "Mom, this is for you because you have been to me—and to many others—what this song describes, and you always will be this to me. Now follow the directions." (My daughter knows me! I am one who reads directions only after I have figured it out for myself but have some pieces left over!) Her instructions were: "1. Get a hankie (maybe two). 2. Find a quiet spot. 3. Play this tape to the end." I obeyed completely. I got my handkerchief, went to our bedroom, plugged in the tape recorder, and listened. It was a beautiful song called "The Wind Beneath My Wings," which spoke of my being a support in my daughter's life, a model as she grew up, and a strength that enabled her to become the woman she is today.

The singer finished, and the next voice was my own dear daughter's saying, "I love you, Mama." It was once again clear to me that Anissa knows her mom well. I needed that handkerchief!

My heart beat wildly and tears of thanksgiving flowed as I realized that my then-19-year-old daughter was acknowledging that I had helped her along the road of life. You and I absolutely never want to jeopardize this precious mother–daughter relationship as we welcome the women whom the Lord sends our way.

Whose Daughter Is She?

Just as we must keep our own daughter aware that she is ours in a very unique and special way and that we will let nothing and no one threaten or alter that relationship, we need to keep in mind that every woman is someone else's daughter in that same special and sacred way. We must always remember to whom she belongs.

All too often a young woman will seek out a strong mother figure because her own mother has not offered her a good model. The parenting she received may not only have been weak but negative and even destructive. Her mother may have hurt her deeply. Abuse can come in a variety of forms, but its wounds always run deep. To help you keep the right perspective on a woman who didn't have godly or healthy parenting, I share with you the rock-solid perspective of my older and very wise friend Mabel.

Mabel and her husband had been married more than 50 years when he died. They raised a family together, worshiped God together, and served Him together. When her dear husband died, Mabel decided to invest herself and some of her time in young women. She has been amazing in this role. Every young woman who enters her life is richly blessed by Mabel's complete and unabashed love for Christ.

In a talk Mabel once gave, she told about a tragedy in her life. She spoke gently with her lovely Canadian accent: "Stan and I lived in a rural area, and our children were born at home. When our second son was born, the doctor came just as we needed him. The delivery was hard, but not too bad. We heard our son cry, and then suddenly—within ten minutes or so—he was dead. Later we learned that the doctor was drunk and, as a result, killed our baby."

People in the room fell silent. Then some women spoke up softly, saying things that would only be asked in this era: "Did you sue?" "I hope he lost his license!" "He should never have delivered another baby!"

Mabel listened to their words and then spoke these simple but profound words: "My God could have saved my baby."

She wasn't bitter or vengeful. She knew her God and His love and power. The measure of her faith and trust in God touched all of us to the very core of our being. When tragedy strikes, how easy it is for us to forget that our omniscient, omnipresent, omnipotent God reigned even as it occurred and that He still reigns. When we come close to another's pain (or even when we're overwhelmed by our own), we can forget He is the Redeemer God, the Romans 8:28 God, the God who shares our sorrows and our hurts.

But Mabel didn't forget who God is, and Mabel's God is the same God who allowed that special but hurting woman whom He sent your way to be raised by her mother and father, whatever pain she experienced in that relationship.

As you share with a woman who has been wounded by her parents, always remember that her loving Creator has plans for her that are good (see Jeremiah 29:11) and that you are in the privileged place of being used by Him, of being an instrument in His hands, as He accomplishes His good.

Then, mindful of the fact that this woman of God is another person's daughter, model Mabel's lack of bitterness and vengefulness. Encourage this sister in the Lord who has been deeply hurt to share openly and honestly her feelings about her lack of parenting. Help her to learn new lessons to replace the wrong ones she was taught and to learn what she never learned as a child. But don't speak against her mother, and never try to take her mother's place. (That advice holds true for any and every mentoring situation, whatever kind of parenting the other woman received.)

Each step of the way, whatever your friend's story, you are to be a model and an encourager, but not a mother. Many of the tasks you perform in the relationship with a younger woman look and feel very much like mothering, but they are not. Your primary goal is to point her in the direction of the Savior. In the case of a woman wounded by her natural mother, your additional goal is to help her establish a relationship with her own mother (see Romans 12:18).

So, as you set forth God's standards for parenting and as you model His plan for motherhood, help your hurting sister identify positive qualities about her own mother. Encourage her to affirm her mother in those areas where she succeeded. Do what you can to lead your friend to a place of reconciliation and peace with her mother. Offer her comfort in her pain but continue to point her in the direction of forgiveness. Indeed, you might have been a "better" mother to her, but you were not the one God chose. He did choose you to be her Titus 2 woman, and that is truly a great honor. What a privilege to be a beacon of God's truth and light, His forgiveness and healing, and to help her find her worth and discover hope in the unconditional and redemptive love of her Creator God and learn how to live a life of holiness that glorifies Him.

The Daughter of a Friend

I was doing a live call-in radio show when a woman phoned, asked several questions, and then, departing from her topic, said, "Donna, if you could give a mother another name, what would it be?" I said a quick prayer for wisdom and, in 30 seconds or so, responded with "facilitator." After all, as mothers we assist our children by giving them full and rich life experiences. We teach them, train them, and, as old Auntie Mame would say, "open new windows" in their lives.

As a mother, I've wanted Anissa to have the rich blessing of knowing my friends and peers. So I encouraged her relationships with those women, and almost all of them were delighted to be a part of my daughter's life—and I was delighted to have them! For instance, since my friend Joan and Anissa have the same temperament, they have loads in common and both especially enjoy poking fun at yours truly! My friend Martha (Anissa called her "Mrs. Martha") did all the domestic things Anissa could never learn from me. My friend Ann happened to be the mother of one of Anissa's high-school chums, and her home was Anissa's home-away-from-home. "Aunt" Mary, who is as different from me as night is from day, nevertheless has the very same belief system and often gave Anissa advice that I wholeheartedly agreed with. In fact, because of this special relationship, Anissa attended Aunt Mary's college alma mater. When Anissa was 15, another friend of mine, who was associated with the missions organization Overseas

Crusade, put us in touch with a family who invited Anissa to spend the summer in France helping missionary families. Anissa cleaned, cooked, baked, cared for the children, assisted in the office, and did any other work she was able to do. Each of these wonderful, unique women—first my friends and then every one a Titus 2 woman for my dear Anissa—brought a dimension into her life that David and I could not. Among other things, they taught her to be accepting of and open to a variety of people. I never felt threatened by their relationships with my daughter. These women were and are my friends. I trusted them with my daughter, and I trusted them to remember the differences between my role in her life and theirs. They invested their lives into hers and consequently find some reward in Anissa's accomplishments.

Such consciousness of the fact that the young woman you are coming alongside is your friend's daughter is crucial when it comes to figuring out how close to draw near. This particular type of relationship is definitely a bit trickier than others God sends our way! Consider that you've probably known this young woman from times when her family and yours got together. This kind of history makes your relationship unique. Then, moving from being a friend to her mother to also being a Titus 2 woman means adding a new dimension to both relationships. Now you are a channel of God's love and guidance to the younger woman in a more personal way.

But being an older woman to this younger woman is often a logical and quite natural relationship. After all, if your style of friendship is like mine or if you were trained by a mother like me, you seldom just take a friend into your life. You also get to know (or at least know about) her husband. You know her grandchildren, her other friends, her parents, her siblings, her heritage—you know her world. Furthermore, the trust that you've established with your friend makes it easier for her to let you get close to her daughter, and that new dimension to the relationship can help your friend as well as her daughter.

I remember Anissa's early years of college when she was redefining her thoughts about men, dating, and marriage and thinking through issues about her appearance. During a meeting with my Chaber group (*chaber* means "bound together" in Hebrew), one of my friends offered to discuss these issues with Anissa over breakfast. During the meal, Naomi shared with Anissa a box shaped like a Bible. Inside it, she had some notes—answers from God's Word—for Anissa to keep. After pointing Anissa to God's Word, Naomi offered her opinions and ideas. Much of what she said Anissa already knew, but hearing it from someone other than dear ol' Mom gave the words of truth new power and significance. I am so thankful for Naomi and her willingness to give her ideas to Anissa.

My generation was eager to take on this kind of responsibility for one another's children. As young mothers, we regularly cared for and even taught our friends' children. When Anissa was little, for example, she and I spent hours with my friend Jan and her son Jeff, who is one year older than Anissa. The little ones played, ate, bathed, and napped together. Being part of such a foursome, I found it easy and natural to say, "No, Jeff. You can't have any more candy." And it was just as easy for Jan to change Anissa's diaper or remind her about the importance of sharing.

Even today, I still stop a child on the street who is damaging property and tell him I am headed for his parents' home to report him. (Old habits die hard!) I believe that children grow to respect adults when we exercise authority in this manner. And I believe that we parents do well to let adults we trust help us raise our children by giving those adults the freedom to exercise authority over our kids and offer godly advice that is consistent with what we have taught them.

During Anissa's college years, she sought advice on a certain matter from one of my friends, and that friend told me of the call before Anissa did. When I later asked Anissa why she hadn't called us, her explanation made perfect sense. She said, "Mom, I know what you and Dad think about this issue. I wanted another opinion—the opinion of someone you and Dad trust." Thinking of her words still brings tears of joy to my eyes and makes me thankful for my friend's presence in Anissa's life as well as my own.

The daughter of a friend may seek you out as Anissa did in this situation. She may want just a single bit of advice, or she may find herself at a shaky point in her life and in need of the additional support of her parents' friends. Whatever the circumstances, the following guidelines will help when your friends' daughters turn to you:

- Let your friend know about your prayerful decision to come alongside her daughter in a Titus 2 way. In some situations, it may be wise to seek your friend's permission before you add this new dimension to your relationship with her daughter.

- Remain loyal to your friend and make sure her daughter knows you will remain a loyal friend to her mother.

- Stay close to your friend during the time you meet with her daughter. Don't give the enemy cause to attack her by preying on any jealous feelings or any sense of rivalry.

- Never blame your friend for whatever circumstances have caused her daughter to turn to you. The situation may or may not be her fault (there are two sides to every story!), but that is God's business. While it is okay and even important for the young woman to share her feelings, never let her speak ill about her mother. Also, demonstrate understanding without allowing disrespect or disobedience.

- Support your friend through your older woman/ younger woman relationship with her daughter, especially if there has been a breach in their relationship.

Throughout your relationship with your friend's daughter, remember that if God has ordained this relationship, you are ultimately helping your friend in her parenting role at the same time that you are helping her daughter. This bond of love for her daughter can deepen your relationship with your friend, and all three of you will benefit. One more thing. As with any Titus 2 relationship, know that fruit is often seen later. Progress may be slow, but be patient. You are doing God's work and He will bless.

Even with the above guidelines, being an older woman to a friend's daughter can be, as I've said, tricky business. I have had failure as well as success in this area, and the failure was very painful. My friend and her daughter were at odds, and encouraging this daughter to be reconciled to her mother was one of my main topics whenever we met. One day, however, the mother approached me and said, "If you weren't in my daughter's life, I feel certain I would be!" Ouch! No one will ever know how those words crushed me. But they also forced me to evaluate my relationship with my friend and with her daughter and to realize that I had broken one of my own rules. I had not stayed close to my friend while I was drawing closer to her daughter.

On a more positive note, I have had the enormous joy of watching a daughter of a friend—a daughter of my heart—become a woman more in love with the Lord. What a privilege! Few experiences match the exhilaration I felt when this young woman came to me and said, "Donna, I need another woman to learn from." There are no problems at all between this woman and her mother. This young woman just needed a different voice at that time, and her mother let me in because she had her daughter's best interest at heart. In fact, my friend said that nothing made her happier than knowing I was praying for her daughter and being a channel of God's love, truth, and guidance. (In fact, it was this friend who helped me formulate the guidelines I shared above for being an older woman to a friend's daughter.)

Let me share another story about drawing close to a friend's daughter. When Martha walked into my heart, she brought her daughters with her. We laughed and played together. They drove my car, wore my clothes, and cared for Anissa. When Martha's daughter Lisa called to tell me she had become officially engaged, we talked about the wedding and she spoke of the place I had in her heart. (As plans for the wedding developed, David and I learned we would be privileged to serve as host and hostess at Lisa and Billy's wedding reception.) Although Lisa—like each of her sisters—is very close to her mother, I have been blessed to play a part in this family that loves and serves God. I have had the opportunity to praise God's works and declare His mighty acts to Martha's daughters (see Psalm 145:4). Martha's girls want my counsel, my ideas, and my help. What a joy and what an honor!

God's Blessed Ways

My mother was angry one day because I wouldn't do what she wanted me to do. Although this scene happened many years ago, I still remember her saying, "If your Aunt Pat asked you to clean the toilet, you'd say, 'How many times?'" Over the years, I've thought about her words. She was probably right, and I don't really understand why the dynamics between mother and daughter are so different from the dynamics between a woman who is her mother's peer and that daughter. I surrender that, with countless other things, to the Isaiah 55:8 category of life ("My thoughts are not your thoughts, neither are your ways My ways....For as the heavens are higher than the earth, so are My ways higher than your ways, and My thoughts than your thoughts"). I don't have any explanation. I just know that our Lord powerfully uses godly older women in the lives of younger women to show them His ways, His truth, and His standards for this life. It was He who ordained and commanded that older women train younger women in the areas of godliness, marriage, mothering, and homemaking. And, as I'm sure you know by now, I feel it's one of the most blessed relationships to be involved in whether you're giving or receiving!

Things to Think About

- If you have been blessed with a daughter, write her a note telling her how very special she is to you.

- In the Old Testament, the suffering Job said of God, "Though he slay me, yet will I trust in him" (Job 13:15 KJV). How well do you do when it comes to trusting God? What verses from the Bible help strengthen your faith when it wavers?

- Think back on a time when you found comfort under God's wings. What did that experience teach you about God? How did it strengthen you to trust in Him?

8
Frustrations and Farewells
Facing the Challenges of the Mentoring Relationship

∼

In 1994, I met a 23-year-old woman from Romania. The mother of three small children, she and her dear husband had opened their home as a residential care facility for the elderly—as his parents had done and their parents before them.

In November of 1994, this young woman's six-month-old baby died in a tragic accident. Her mother, her husband's mother, her sisters, and her friends were there with her, and they helped her through this time of pain and grief. But in a conversation just weeks after the funeral, she thanked me for the message of hope I was able to bring. As an older woman in her life—not a family member or a peer—I occupy a unique place in her life. God used me to meet a need that another young friend and even her own mother could not meet. And He can use you in the very same way to give to another of His daughters exactly what she needs.

Each of us, however, will give differently because each of us is one of God's unique creations and because each woman He brings into òur lives for this special Titus 2 relationship is also a precious, one-of-a-kind creation of the King. Some relationships will be challenging, as we will discuss in this chapter. Some relationships will last only a short season. Some will become friendships for life. Given the uniqueness of us human beings, our personal style of friendships, and our distinct personalities, relationships with one another can vary widely.

A Woman Who Refines Us

"Oh, no. Here she comes again. If only she weren't such an incessant chatterbox, forever asking questions that have already been answered....If only she would listen....Lord, perhaps You could send a distraction and change her path. No, here she comes."

You probably wouldn't expect thoughts like these to run through the mind of a woman of God as the woman God has brought into her life approaches. But thoughts like these do in fact come when we are sent a woman we may not want—specifically, a woman God sends to refine us. And I hope my honesty doesn't offend, but I speak of this kind of relationship because I have been a difficult daughter of the heart and because God has sent such a daughter of the heart to me.

Let me share about the time I was a difficult daughter of the heart. I remember, for instance, times when I knew all too clearly what I should do in a given situation. God had made it clear to me, but I didn't want to take action. (It's so much easier just to talk forever and forever about the issues rather than to act on them, isn't it?) I know now that I called this dear woman too often and tried to find an easy way around her very direct responses to my questions. I am certain by the tone of her voice and her husband's that, although I know they loved me, there were times they wished I would just go away. In circumstances like these, it's important to determine if the pursuing and/or irritating woman is being sent to you by God. If so, what are you to do with her?

First, keep in mind that in some cases a woman of God is sought after because she has power, influence, wealth, education, heritage, fame, notoriety, a contagious sense of fun, a famous husband, a husband who is a pastor, or because her ministry to other women has been so positive that many others want to be close to her. A woman who is sought after for any of these reasons—and you may be in such a position—needs to realize that she cannot possibly make time for every woman who writes or calls her. Only God can direct you to the woman in whom He would have you invest time and energy. You must know His voice and then be obedient to what He instructs. And, actually, such confidence that the Lord is bringing a particular woman into your life so that you can pass on your knowledge of and love for Him is key to any Titus 2 relationship between women of God. His direction, His guidance, and His voice—this is how we know if a woman (difficult or delightful) is the one with whom God would have us share our lives.

Now on to the second point. If God is clearly sending this difficult woman into your life, how are you to handle her?

First, remember that God's plan for us is always best and that the methods He uses to refine us are His business, not ours. When the Lord first gave me a difficult daughter of the heart, I realized that she was there to teach me. But would I be teachable? Would I let myself be taught, refined, sharpened by this woman God had sent to me? The decision to receive this gift from my heavenly Father was mine alone.

I did receive this young woman, and that's when the Lord changed my exasperation with her. He did so by opening my eyes to my own behavior toward one of the older women earlier in my life. God forced me to acknowledge my insensitivity to family times in her home and the occasions when I had taken too many liberties. He showed me how I had usurped her time and disregarded her boundaries. This look back at my life forced me to answer God's question to me about the difficult daughter of the heart He was sending me—"Donna, what were you like at her age?"—and then to accept her and extend to her His love and compassion.

When God sends a difficult, troublesome, or irritating woman your way, He also provides the love and grace you need to be able to be a beacon of His light to her. Keep in mind that you receive God's grace and His love for this difficult woman when you pray. In fact, "pray" is the best one-word answer to the question, "What do I do with this troublesome or irritating person?" Pray for her—and pray for yourself and the lessons God would have you learn from her. (As you see God answer this ongoing prayer, you will realize that God often uses such a woman in your life more than He uses you in hers!)

And what are some of the lessons, by God's grace, a difficult daughter of the heart will help teach you? Well, she will teach you the importance of relying on the Lord by keeping you on your knees and humble before Him. She will also teach you to set and maintain boundaries (but know going into this that a difficult daughter of your heart will test every boundary you set!).

In *Ordering Your Private World*, Gordon MacDonald tells about being in his study one Saturday, the day he set aside for final sermon preparation. When the phone rang, he answered it. The woman on the other end was clearly upset and said, "I must see you now! It's urgent." Being young, he stopped his final sermon preparation and went to the church to meet her. When he got there he discovered that this difficulty had been going on for many years.

The next time he got a call like this, he immediately asked how long the caller had been dealing with the situation. After learning that it was not an emergency, Pastor MacDonald explained that he would be preaching three times the next day, was occupied with his sermon, and would be unable to give the caller his total attention. He then said, "Since this has been going on for several years, it can wait until Monday. Call me in the morning and we'll set up an appointment." He had realized that he would be the one to blame if he let others rob him of his time—and the same is true for you and me. Remember that there is time enough to do all that God wants us to do.

So what will you do if this difficult woman calls at dinnertime? Be firm and tell her you will have time for her tomorrow. If she asks for 10 minutes and you're certain she'll take 20, respond with, "You know how easy it is to talk longer than 10 minutes! I'll set my timer to help us stay on track." Such responses are not rejection. They are a way of training a difficult daughter of the heart and helping her learn lessons for life at the same time that you use your time wisely.

A Faltering Daughter of the Heart

A young woman who wants help but is so weak she hardly knows where to begin offers different relational challenges. This woman knows that she needs you, you hear God calling you to be there for her, and so the two of you start meeting together. But it's not long until you are completely frustrated. This woman's life skills are so poor and her experience in right living so minimal that, no matter what happens in life and no matter how you coach her, she seems to fall off the log.

Delores was just such a woman. When she first came to our Mentors for Mothers program, her hair was often dirty, matted, and uncombed. She always wore dark clothes (to hide the dirt?), and her shoes were never polished. Most distressing was her cynical attitude toward life and her skepticism about whether the Bible's values, standards, and guidelines could work in real life. Could a godly woman who lived according to the Lord's Word really make it? "After all," she often said, "this is the nineties!" And this woman, you say, was in Mentors for Mothers? Yes, because we only have two requirements: The moms have to want to come and demonstrate that by faithfully attending, and the mentors have to love Jesus. Delores met the requirement: Her surprisingly (to us) faithful attendance clearly showed us that she really wanted to come.

Problems arose early for Delores and her mentor. First, Delores desired far greater change than she was able to accomplish. She desperately wanted to change. She saw young women eager for God; she wasn't. She saw good marriages; hers was in a shambles. She heard about neat homes; hers was a disaster. Despite these grand goals, her mentor saw very little progress at all. Furthermore, Delores poked fun at her mentor's "corny" ideas about family life. Her skepticism seemed to make her deaf to anything her mentor said. Still, the mentor stayed faithful, listening and offering assistance whenever she could, praying for and loving this young woman whom she knew God had sent.

Well, at the end of the Mentors for Mothers year, dear Delores rose to her feet. Her hair was clean and combed, and she wore a bright floral dress, pearls at her neck, and a new pair of beige shoes on her feet. Tears fell like rain from my eyes as I listened to her explain what the past 12 months had done for her. (Her physical appearance told all of us a great deal even before she opened her mouth!) First, Delores affirmed the steadfastness of her mentor. She also explained that the word *friend* was not one she threw around easily, but she could most certainly say that her mentor had become her friend. Then Delores ended by saying, "I realize I haven't accomplished in these 12 months all I hoped to—and certainly not as much as my mentor had hoped I would. But I will take with me, for the rest of my life, the godly attributes I saw her live out." She was changed in the presence of a holy God.

So don't despair over a faltering young woman. Walk with her and let her grow at her speed. After all, we must have different standards for each person, and your standards for someone who is faltering need to fit her. Say what you feel God wants you to say. Sow the seed of His truth and His Word. Do what you can to nurture that seed, but trust the harvest to Him. Also, trust this faltering sister to Him. Trust that God is at work in her heart despite what you are seeing or not seeing. He doesn't give up on any of us, so don't give up on her.

Relationships for a Season

"Messenger of Sympathy and Love, Servant of Parted Friends"—these words are part of the motto etched above the portals of the U.S. Post Office in Washington, D.C. And these words are especially meaningful when we consider women of God who are with us only for a season.

It's a bittersweet fact that women we draw close to may not stay in our lives forever. So cherish the time you have with them. At the same time, don't cling or let their growth or dependency on you become your sole source of affirmation. (That's God's role!) Following these two guidelines will make letting go easier when the time comes. You—and she—will probably still shed some tears, but among the tears of sadness at parting will be tears of joy for what you two have been able to share.

I know about tears when it comes to saying goodbye, for I had to say goodbye to Wendy. When I met Wendy in a Bible-study class I was teaching in my church, I saw right away that we were kindred spirits. We struck up an instant friendship that, rooted in Christ's love, quickly deepened.

Wise for her years and eager to be all she could be in Christ, Wendy sought my advice in the very areas God calls us older women to give advice in. She was quick to challenge me, and I was just as quick to make certain my information was accurate. She also helped me understand more about the pressures an educated older mother feels and how she makes her decisions. She taught me much during our time together.

After a few years, she and her husband decided to go to the mission field for two years, and that step seemed perfect for their family. I felt sad when they left, but Wendy's letters were frequent. She also visited and called when they were in the States on furlough.

At the end of their two years of missions work, Wendy's family headed home to a house that we knew had been poorly maintained by the tenants. With the help of many of their friends and a few of mine, their home was transformed by new carpeting, new curtains, new furniture, and new paint from top to bottom. When the family arrived home, their own books were in the bookcase and their family photos on the table.

Welcome back, daughter of my heart! I thought. But within six months her husband decided to move his family to another state and change careers. This time I faced letting go permanently—except through the mail.

Standing True to God's Call

Like any work we do, ministering as a Titus 2 woman will have its frustrations as well as its joys, its happy moments as well as its sad ones. When God sends us a woman to help refine us and make us more Christlike, the Titus 2 ministry can be especially challenging. When He sends a faltering daughter our way, the ministry can be discouraging. And when He shows us that it's time to say goodbye to one we've come to love, our ministry can become quite bittersweet.

Therefore, throughout our Titus 2 relationships—and they'll be as rich and varied as God's daughters themselves are—we do well to make the words of the following hymn our heartfelt commitment and prayer.

I Would Be True

I would be true, for there are those who trust me;
I would be pure, for there are those who care;
I would be strong, for there is much to suffer;
I would be brave, for there is much to dare,
I would be brave, for there is much to dare.

I would be friend of all, the foe, the friendless;
I would be giving, and forget the gift;
I would be humble, for I know my weakness;
I would look up and laugh and love and lift,
I would look up and laugh and love and lift.

—HOWARD ARNOLD WALTER

Our heavenly Father will indeed honor such a woman of God who says, "Here am I! Use me in the life of the precious child You send my way" and then keeps her eyes on Him as she serves. Always remember that difficult, faltering, or distant, the joy of being involved with a fellow sojourner is enormous.

Things to Think About

- We are called to be stewards of our time as well as our treasures and our talents. How are you spending your days? What does last week's calendar reveal about your priorities? What good things did you do? What better things could you have been doing?

- In what area of your life do you most struggle with setting boundaries? Why do you struggle with setting boundaries? To whom can you go for support (prayer and practical) and accountability?

- How do you usually respond to someone who is slow to catch on to what you are saying or teaching? How would you like to respond to a slow student? How would Jesus want you to respond? How can He help you do so?

- When has someone you loved moved away? What feelings did you have when you said goodbye, and how did you deal with them?

9

Rave Reviews

Celebrating the Blessings of the Titus 2 Ministry

~

When I was a child, one of my favorite pastimes was reading. I had an especially hard time putting down the biographies and autobiographies I opened. Perhaps even as a child I enjoyed watching through the pages of a book how people lived and learning why they did what they did. Although these men and women were leaps and bounds ahead of me in character and faith, I knew that in some ways each of them was just like me, and this realization stimulated me to good deeds.

During the late eighties, I had the opportunity to hear author and speaker Jean Lush. As I listened to this delightful woman, her elderly face framed by beautiful white hair, I was amazed by the frankness with which this woman—at least 30 years my senior—spoke. It was absolutely exhilarating. Thirty minutes into her message, it hit me. When you get old or older, you can say a lot more than you were able to say when you were young. I'd found yet another reason to celebrate growing older.

A few months later I talked to Elisabeth Elliot Gren about my observation. "Is it true that as you get older you are able to say more than you did when you were young?" I asked. Elisabeth, who is nearly 20 years older than me, stated in true Elisabeth style, "Certainly," and promptly sent me the following piece:

Prayer for the Middle-Aged
By a 17ᵗʰ-Century Nun

Lord, Thou knowest better than I know myself
that I am growing old.
Keep me from the fatal habit of thinking
I must say something on every subject
and on every occasion.

Release me from craving to straighten out everybody's affairs.
Make me thoughtful but not moody, helpful but not bossy.
With my vast store of wisdom it seems a pity
not to use it all, but Thou knowest, Lord,
that I want a few friends at the end.

Keep my mind free from the recital of endless details;
give me wings to get to the point.
Seal my lips on my aches and pains.
They are increasing, and love of rehearsing them is
becoming sweeter as the years go by.

I dare not ask for grace enough to enjoy the tales of others' pains,
but help me to endure them with patience.
I dare not ask for improved memory, but
for a growing humility and a lessening cocksureness when
my memory seems to clash with the memories of others.

Teach me the glorious lesson that occasionally
I may be mistaken.

Keep me reasonably sweet.
I do not want to be a saint—
some of them are so hard to live with—
but a sour old person is one of the crowning works of the devil.

Give me the ability to see good things in unexpected places
and talents in unexpected people.
Give me the grace to tell them so.

Amen.

I, too, say "amen" to that prayer! Don't you?

Letters of Today

Like our prayers, our letters can reveal much about us. That's why I want to share with you some letters from older women who have shared themselves and their faith with other (usually younger) women of God. Having talked to these women, I know how timid they were about reaching out. But before they took their first step, I also knew they would be blessed if they did so—yet not even I expected the blessings to be so great.

> I wanted to help somewhere in the church. The young woman I received was brand-new in her walk. I could answer every one of her questions with assurance. It made me realize just how much I knew about God and His Word.

> After meeting my daughter of the heart, I wondered what God had in mind. I knew she was young and I was old, but I also saw her strengths and her love for God and family. I could not find any holes in her armor, so to speak. It took only about six weeks until I realized that God had sent me to pray for her

> and with her. She regularly remarked, "I have learned so much about praying."
>
> I have often struggled with, "What can I, at 70, offer anyone?" I now know. This passage in Titus talks about what I know best—being a Christian, a wife (I've been one for 52 years), a mother, and sharing my home with others. I have time in my world for more than one young woman, and I am going to do this kind of work until I die.

This dear woman died two years after she wrote this letter. When I spoke with her in the hospital, she was so pleased with God's leading in her life. I shall never forget her comment: "I went to help her, and she helped me much more." And what about this letter:

> I figured after 46 years of marriage I had all the answers. However, as the young woman in my life asked me questions about marriage, submission, intimacy, and building her husband up, I came face-to-face with the fact that I needed to do some learning, too. So we learned together, we prayed together, and we saw some changes together. It was very sweet.

Words from the Younger Women

What younger women have said may also help give you a more up-close-and-personal understanding of what a Titus 2 ministry is all about and what it can mean to the women God puts in your life.

How grateful I am that I followed the persistent prompting to get involved in the life of an older woman. How very, very faithful is the Father for He knew my need to be in her presence, to be nourished by her deep well of wisdom, spiritually and experientially. She has encouraged me to fix my eyes on what is eternal and what is a lasting treasure—Jesus.

When I first met my older woman, I was expecting my third child. Daily I felt exhausted and overwhelmed. Then my mentor arrived with love, knowledge, and encouragement. I wanted so desperately to know some practical and biblical applications to being a wife, a mother, a housekeeper, a cook—all the things I was doing at home but without godly insight. She truly set me on the track to being a Proverbs 31 woman. I will never ever be able to thank her for everything she gave me.

The voice of an experienced, godly woman saying what I already believed in my heart to be true about the value of being a keeper of my home, a lover of my husband, and the primary caregiver of my children validated my convictions. I am eternally grateful for her life-changing influence, and I hope to pass that same influence on to the next generation.

(Rereading this letter makes me want to jump up and down! Hooray for her and for her Titus 2 woman!)

You bring to mind heart and home. Your enjoyment of cooking for your family inspires the thought of the kitchen and hearth being the center of the home. The Proverbs 31 woman also provided for her family. She also had a husband who trusted in her, and I have seen this trust between Dick and you. Thank you for being an example to me in these most important areas of family life.

A Chance to Learn

Are all Titus 2 relationships talked about so glowingly? To be honest, I do on very rare occasions hear about a negative experience. When I do, I find those letters important teachers for those of us who respond to God's Titus 2 commands. As an example, let me share some comments from one such letter: "I was so disappointed in my older woman. She was tardy, did not keep her word, and finally admitted she did not have time for me."

A year after I received that letter, I heard from the writer again: "I have given much thought to my frank note of last year. One year later I realize that, although my dream of what a relationship with an older woman would be (I do have a woman in my life now) was dashed, the disappointment taught me a very valuable lesson. I don't want to be old and late in appointments or not able to prioritize my time. I am grateful for what I saw. It taught me what I did not want to be."

God used even this disappointing relationship with an older woman of God to teach the younger woman who watched her some valuable lessons. And of course He uses the rewarding older woman/younger woman relationships to benefit those involved—and their family members as well. Let me close with this delightful example. When a young woman was perplexed about how to handle a given situation in the home, her husband told her, "Call your mentor!" The older woman's positive influence on his wife had so impressed him that he suggested calling her before calling his folks or his wife's!

I hope these letters and stories inspire you because I realize that the charge of Titus 2 can seem overwhelming. Upon reading Paul's words, you may feel that there's only a dim chance that you could ever fulfill the ministry he describes. But as these letters show, you can and, with God's blessing, *will* be used by Him to encourage other women in their efforts to be a woman whose life honors Him. In fact, the younger women He calls you to mentor may be feeling there's only a dim chance they can manage all that life entails, but you—by your very presence and due to the fact that you've lived through many of the challenges they now face—will offer them the bright hope that they can and will survive. It's a vital ministry, and it's one that God will enable you to do and do well. Take the step of faith and see!

Things to Think About

- Write a letter to God and tell Him what you hear as His call to you personally in Titus 2, your concerns about responding to that call, and your hopes for a ministry of coming alongside a woman of God to share your knowledge of Him. Let this letter be a prayer as well as a touchstone for you in the future when you are being a Titus 2 woman.

10
The Fingerprint of God

*Continuing to be Touched by God's
Transforming Power*

~

As we've seen throughout this book, women who model their lives on Titus 2:3-5 become *messengers of God's love* to the next generation and often to their own peers. And through the years I've seen that these older women share certain other common characteristics—evidence of God's fingerprints on their lives. A review of the following traits will serve as a reminder that ministry happens between women of God not because older women have crossed some spiritual finish line, but because they are being touched by the Lord's transforming power day by day.

A Heart for God

First and foremost, a woman who has walked with the Lord through the years knows to look for God in all people and all circumstances and knows how to see Him when she looks. This godly woman allows God to truly rule her days, her hours, her minutes. She practices His presence, rests in His lordship, and abides in His love. This kind of heart for God is granted to all who seek Him, and this kind of heart for God makes an older woman a gracious channel of His love for those of us blessed by her presence in our life.

A Teachable Spirit

One of my favorite people in Scripture is Apollos, and you might not even be acquainted with him. We don't hear a lot about him or his work. Most often he is just referred to when members of the early Christian community are asked, "Are you of Apollos or Paul?" Apollos takes center stage, however, in a brief passage in the book of Acts:

> Now a certain Jew named Apollos, an Alexandrian by birth, an eloquent man, came to Ephesus; and he was mighty in the Scriptures. This man had been instructed in the way of the Lord; and being fervent in spirit, he was speaking and teaching accurately the things concerning Jesus, being acquainted only with the baptism of John; and he began to speak out boldly in the synagogue. But when Priscilla and Aquila heard him, they took him aside and explained to him the way of God more accurately.
>
> And when he wanted to go across to Achaia, the brethren encouraged him and wrote to the disciples to welcome him; and when he had arrived, he helped greatly those who had believed through grace; for he powerfully refuted the Jews in public, demonstrating by the Scriptures that Jesus was the Christ (18:24-28).

Notice how this man Apollos is described. He's eloquent, "mighty in the Scriptures," "fervent in spirit," and able to speak and teach accurately. We would do well to have any one of those traits, much less all of them! But the little word that points out Apollos's most desirable trait is the word more at the end of verse 26.

Here's the situation: Priscilla and Aquila come to town and hear Apollos teach. After he is finished, they go up to him and say, "You need to present God's Word more accurately than you already are." Despite his strong credentials and proven effectiveness, Apollos hears what they say and, evidenced by the fact that his ministry continued with the strong support of his fellow believers, apparently agrees and learns and changes. Apollos is teachable. That is the trait I most admire about him—and the one I most want for myself!

Older women who are becoming God's messengers to the next generation know their message on the Lord's behalf, but they also know the Lord isn't finished with them yet. They know that He will continue to teach them until they go home to be with Him. They are teachable and willing to learn from people of all ages.

Martha was one of God's messengers in my life who was indeed teachable. She was also the answer to a prayer I prayed as I moved back to Chicago. My experiences with older women had been rich up to that point, and now at the age of 27 I expected this pattern to continue. In fact, in my prayers I offered God a list of desirable qualities in the older women He had for me there. I specified that these older women should be intelligent, educated, married, orderly, the manager of an efficient and effective home, interested in art, history, and music, the mother of well-behaved children, and active in their church and community life. I was so arrogant. As if I knew what I needed to make me more a woman after God's own heart!

In response to my prayers, God wisely sent me Martha. Now she had many of the qualities I was looking for, but some important (in my mind) traits were missing. When I went to Martha's home, for instance, we had to move the pile of clean clothes waiting to be folded before we could sit on the sofa for a visit ("the manager of an efficient and effective home"?). Born and raised in the hills of Arkansas, Martha had a high school education ("educated"?). Her interest in art was marginal, and with five daughters she had little time for community activity.

But of course God knew exactly what He was doing when He placed her in my life. Daily, Martha lived out her love for God: She was a friend to many, she spoke forth her beliefs whenever she had an opportunity, and she befriended women, young and old alike. Above all, though, Martha was teachable. She taught me many things as I watched her, and I clearly saw that she was always learning something new. I also realized that I wanted that trait in my life. I was changed forever because Martha allowed herself to be a messenger of the Lord. I was lost when Martha, acting as God's messenger, swooped me up in her arms and offered me everyday lessons on each of the Titus 2 concepts. I am forever grateful she did so.

The Lord's Perspective of Time

While many people live primarily in the past, present, or future, a messenger for God understands that we are never to dwell too long in any one of those time zones. Looking too much at the past can cause us to get stuck on the pain or wax nostalgic for the "good ol' days." Thinking only of the present can look a lot like eating, drinking, and being merry and then having nothing of eternal value to show for our lives when they come to an end. And looking only to the future can lead us to miss the gift of the present as we plan for a tomorrow that may never come. Understanding time and the interconnection of past, present, and future causes us to remember God's faithfulness in the past, enjoy His gift of the present, anticipate His redemptive coming again, and celebrate the truth that "Jesus Christ is the same yesterday and today, yes and forever" (Hebrews 13:8). What a testimony such an understanding is!

Having our heavenly Father's perspective on time also means realizing that we are to invest in the next generation of His people. With this heaven-bound rather than earth-bound mind-set, God's messengers are aware that everything they do and say affects future generations (statistics tell us for four generations!).

A Willingness to Share Their Knowledge of God

Jesus' great commission to share the good news of God's forgiving love and to make disciples of all nations (Matthew 28:19) is a command to you and me, not a special assignment strictly for trained public speakers, Bible teachers, ordained pastors, and gifted evangelists. Each one of us is called to know our faith and be able to explain and defend it (1 Peter 3:15). And, as we've seen in Paul's words to Titus, we who are older are instructed specifically to pass our knowledge of our God on to our younger sisters in the faith. On occasion, doing so may mean speaking up for what is right when no one else will.

> *I spoke*
> *Words fell*
> *Aimlessly on ears.*
> *Later*
> *One said,*
> *"Your word—*
> *It helped*
> *That day."*

I turned
Wondering—
Forgot I said
That word.
Let me speak
Those words
Often.
Helpful words
That I forget.

—JIM ELIOT in *The Journals of Jim Eliot*

When a friend was in the middle of an enormously unpleasant divorce, a couple who had been longtime friends came alongside her. The husband offered to escort my friend to some social gatherings. Although the relationship was purely platonic, she nevertheless asked this question at lunch one day: "Should I continue to attend public functions with him?" A very shy and usually very quiet woman spoke up without hesitation. "No," she said simply but firmly, "I believe our appearances and our actions should be above reproach." There was a holy hush in that room. It takes courage to speak forth words like those, and a person who clearly knows what she believes finds that courage.

A Loving Commitment to People

John D. Rockefeller once said, "I would pay any price for a man who was able to get along with others." Living in relationship, in harmony with the people around us, is not easy for us human beings. That's why Christian community can be such a testimony in our world. After all, didn't Jesus command us to love one another (Mark 12:31)? And doesn't the Bible teach that people will know us as God's people by our love for one another (John 13:35)? Such love means standing by difficult people, staying with someone for the long haul, and asking God to give us hearts that accept the people we encounter and eyes to see Jesus in them. Being in relationship with people means being a channel of God's grace in the world.

A Willingness to Extend Warm Hospitality

My Aunt Pat was one of the most influential people in my life. She didn't finish high school, and she never held more than a parttime waitressing job in the dining room of a private law association. Aunt Pat's influence came not from a fine education or a powerful, prestigious position. Her influence on me came as she cooked, sewed, baked, and served her church and her community. Her influence came as she personified hospitality.

Every time I went to Aunt Pat's home, a wonderful smell from the kitchen greeted me—lemon pound cake, freshly baked bread, the spices of Assyrian food. The table in her kitchen table often had on it a huge floral tablecloth. It didn't matter who you were or what time of day or night you arrived. She made everyone feel welcome and accepted. Within minutes, you had something to eat or drink in your hand despite the fact that in those days my aunt and uncle didn't know anything about "extra" money in a bank account. Dear Aunt Pat made me want to cook, bake, crochet, embroider, be hospitable, love others—in a word, *imitate* her. She was a model, a messenger, an older woman God placed in my life to help me enter adulthood. Her lessons about the value of hospitality went straight to my heart.

Availability, Acceptance, and Affirmation

A classic example of an older woman being there for a younger woman in a Titus 2 relationship is found in the relationship between Elizabeth and Mary. Where did young Mary go when she learned from the angel that she, a virgin engaged to be married, was carrying God's Son in her womb? She went straight to her older cousin Elizabeth. Now remember that in her day Mary could have been stoned for being pregnant. At the very least she could be ostracized and cast away. What would happen to her planned marriage? Would Joseph believe her account of the angel and God's message? Clearly, these early days of pregnancy may not have been very comfortable or easy for Mary for a variety of emotional as well as physical reasons. So Mary went to Elizabeth, and Elizabeth received her warmly. Elizabeth was lovingly available, she wholeheartedly accepted and welcomed her cousin (just as the cartwheeling baby in her own womb welcomed the baby in Mary's!), and she affirmed the wondrous privilege Mary had of being chosen by God for a special purpose.

Availability, acceptance, and affirmation—a woman of God can give these to another woman. Other people in her life can be critics; she needs a cheerleader. Others can try to force her toward their goals for her; she needs to be loved for who she is and what she dreams. Others can be busy with their own things; she wants someone who will simply spend some time with her. Others will be too busy talking to ever listen; she needs someone eager to hear her. Other women might try to make her a mirror image of themselves; she needs a woman who will help her become the person God has called her to be. In fact, that's one of the primary motives of a godly woman who walks alongside another woman.

A heart for God, a teachable spirit, the Lord's perspective on time, a solid knowledge of their faith, the ability and boldness to share their beliefs, a commitment to people, a warm hospitality for all who come their way, a loving availability, and an accepting, affirming spirit—these are the traits of the woman of God, the Titus woman, the older woman who can make a difference for God's kingdom by passing on His truth and His values to the next generation. What motivates such a woman to draw alongside another woman, a younger woman? She doesn't do it to earn another jewel in her crown. She's not seeking a substitute daughter or trying to clone herself. She's not opting for an easy "out" when it comes to serving God. (This ministry can, in fact, be as costly as it is rewarding!) No, a godly woman is simply acting out of obedience to God's clearly stated command in Titus 2. She is giving away what she has and who she is, she is imparting God's truth and extending fond affection, she is being Jesus with skin and bones to the women to whom God calls her to reach out.

As I've studied Titus 2 and listened for God's direction, I've been guided by the words of Elisabeth Elliot Gren: "God ordained that I participate." God ordained this older woman/younger woman relationship—these blessed relationships between women of God—so that you and I would participate. Elisabeth helped me see that God does His work and I am to do mine. The Lord doesn't say, "I hope you follow My plan." He says, "Follow it!"

Is your life in order so that you can obey? Are you listening for God's specific instructions to you? Is your heart open so that you will hear where He leads and then go where He directs? His commandment is issued to you— and His blessings await when you respond!

Things to Think About

- Read the verses that follow. How do they encourage you in your walk with the Lord?

   —When Thou didst say, "Seek My face," my heart said to Thee, "Thy face, O LORD, I shall seek" (Psalm 27:8).

— And I will give them a heart to know Me, for I am the LORD; and they will be My people, and I will be their God, for they will return to Me with their whole heart (Jeremiah 24:7).

— As for you, my son Solomon, know the God of your father, and serve Him with a whole heart and a willing mind; for the Lord searches all hearts, and understands every intent of the thoughts. If you seek Him, He will let you find Him... (1 Chronicles 28:9).

— The young lions do lack and suffer hunger; but they who seek the Lord shall not be in want of any good thing (Psalm 34:10).

• How can you cultivate the traits listed in this chapter?

11
Our Privilege
Titus 2 in Action

∽

*I*t was Sunday morning. As we had done every week for years, my husband and I went to our classroom at church to teach the 50 faithful couples who attend "Family Circles." These bright, educated young men and women love God, one another, and us.

But this Sunday was not a typical one. Less than 24 hours earlier, my husband's father had died at the age of 88. When David and I discussed whether we should go to class, we decided the best place for us to be was at the house of God with people who love Him as we do.

As David stood before the men and women who had prayed with us and for us through the 12 months of Poppa Otto's decline, he described the previous 24 hours, Poppa's strained breathing, his last minutes, and plans for his final resting place.

When David finished, a young man rose to his feet and said, "Could a few men gather around David and pray for him?" I will never forget that image of not a few but all of the men in the class rising quickly and surrounding David. Tears filled my eyes as I saw these men honor their father in the faith. Their fervent prayers revealed their love, concern, and respect for David. Later in the day, David told me it took all of his physical strength to stand erect under the force of the men's hands on his shoulders. What a powerful reminder of God's love!

And those reminders continued in the days that followed as these dear young friends sent cards and flowers, brought meals, attended the memorial service, ran errands, drove us to the airport—did anything they could to demonstrate their love and support. David and I were very touched and very blessed.

I couldn't help but think of what God said to Ruth when He gave her a son: "May he also be to you a restorer of life and a sustainer of your old age" (Ruth 4:15). These sons and daughters in the faith certainly were restoring and sustaining us. I also thought of Jesus' words: "Behold, My mother and My brothers! For whoever does the will of My Father who is in heaven, he is My brother and sister and mother" (Matthew 12:49,50). These dear young friends are indeed family, and David and I thank God for them.

Family Duty, Family Privilege

Prepared to read a passage of Scripture and say a few words at the memorial service for her grandfather, our daughter Anissa stood at the podium. When she saw the number of young faces in the congregation, her first words were "I'm an only daughter who lives away from her parents. I know that it is you who comfort and care for my parents. Thank you."

With that simple statement, David and I realized then that the young men and women in our world—in Family

Circles, in Mentors for Mothers, in Homemakers by Choice, in Lilies, and in Study Sisters—were the sons and daughters of our hearts. They were indeed God's family—our family—and they did, as Anissa recognized, support and care for us in a multitude of ways. And that's exactly what our heavenly Father planned for us. As His family, we are to care for one another.

And one way we older members of the family care for younger members (and even our peers) is by sharing with them our knowledge of God and His Word. Just as each generation of Israel declared to the next the faithfulness of God through accounts of the Passover, the Red Sea parting, the exodus from Egypt, the manna sent from heaven, the guiding cloud by day and the blazing fire by night, we who are the new Israel—God's children, heirs with Christ—are to share our own testimonies of His faithfulness.

In my 55 years of living, I have indeed seen God be faithful again and again, in the big things and the little things, in my life and in the lives of others. And this witness is an important gift for us to give to other believers, especially to younger people struggling with the challenges of life which we have already faced. It is so important that, as we have seen in our study of Titus 2, God commands that we do so. Look again at God's call to you:

> Older women likewise are to be reverent in their behavior, not malicious gossips, nor enslaved to much wine, teaching what is good, that they may encourage the young women to love their husbands, to love their children, to be sensible, pure, workers at home, kind, being subject to their own husbands, that the word of God may not be dishonored (Titus 2:3-5).

Being a Titus 2 woman, a spiritual mother, a beacon of God's love takes time and energy. It means risk. It calls you to be vulnerable and open. So why do it? Because God commands it and so "that the word of God will not be dishonored." You know God and His Word. To not share that hard-won, lifelong knowledge would indeed dishonor Him and His truth. Furthermore, the hours, the energy, the prayer, the love you invest in some of God's precious daughters will not only please the King of kings, but it will also mean a great blessing for you as you draw closer to these members of His family.

Obedience, Joy, and Blessing

God commands. God calls. And when He calls, He equips. There's no reason for any of us to hold back from the Titus 2 ministry that is part of the good Lord's plan. So be a doer of the Word, not just a hearer (James 1:22)—but don't wait too long! (Remember the virgins in Matthew 25:1-10 who didn't have their lamps ready, and, as a result, missed the wedding feast when the bridegroom came?)

You and I certainly have the freedom to say no to God. We do so all the time. But don't say no! Don't miss the blessing! God's Titus 2 design, His older woman–younger woman plan, is intended to bless you as much as it blesses your sisters in the faith. (In fact, on occasion, I'm sure I've been far more blessed than my daughter of the heart!)

So accept God's call. Respond to His call to this special ministry with prayer, with His love for the woman He sends your way, and with the confidence that He will use you whatever your strengths and weaknesses, whatever your joys and struggles, whatever your story, whatever your dreams.

Don't underestimate how God will use you or the gifts He has given you to share. Instead, love the way you can love—with encouragement, perspective, and wisdom. That kind of love is just what your sisters in Christ—whatever their ages—need and want! Furthermore, your obedience will mean joy and blessing beyond expectation. As you pass on the passions of your life and the convictions of your heart, you will indeed be blessed at the same time the Lord uses you to bless one of His precious daughters. It is my prayer that, as you minister in this crucial and life-changing way, you will join with Paul in saying,

> *Having thus a fond affection for you,*
> *we were well-pleased to impart to you*
> *not only the gospel of God but also our own lives.*

—1 THESSALONIANS 2:8

Tools for Developing Successful Mentoring Relationships

A Touch of Grace

A Visit with Elisabeth Elliot Gren

~

When I was in my early thirties, God sent an older woman into my life who has had a profound effect on my understanding of godliness and what can happen between women of God. When I met author Elisabeth Elliot Gren, I knew right away that she offered me a model of godliness and could teach me much. In fact, she is that kind of model to literally hundreds of thousands of women through her books and radio broadcasts.

I'm hardly alone in thinking of Elisabeth as a spiritual mother. But perhaps because of my track record in drawing close to and learning from older women, perhaps because of my persevering nature, and perhaps because Elisabeth wanted to help me, she has been an important "older woman" to me in the Titus 2 sense of the phrase. Many years ago I asked Elisabeth if she would be willing to teach me and help me be a woman of God. I have watched her closely as she has taught other women and managed her home and her life. Moment by moment and day by day, her life truly reflects the messages she shares in her books and public appearances, and it offers many lessons to those of us who have had the opportunity to watch her up close as well as from afar.

Older Woman, Younger Woman

In 1988, Elisabeth and I had one of several discussions about the older woman of Titus 2:3-5. I was trying to come up with a way to refer to this special woman. Elisabeth suggested, "How about the WOTTs woman—the Woman of Titus Two?" Now, whenever I think of that older woman whom Paul describes in Titus, I smile and think of Elisabeth and her term straight from Scripture!

I recently asked Elisabeth what she thinks of the nineties term *mentor* as a synonym for a WOTTs woman. Pointing out that *mentor* is a broader term than we have in mind, she continued:

> Anybody—man or woman—can be a mentor. I think of myself as an "older woman" because it is a biblical term. We need not limit it to chronological age. A younger woman may be more mature spiritually than a woman who is older chronologically.
>
> I remind young women who longingly wish for an older woman in their life, "You are supposed to be a spiritual mother too. Spend more time asking God to qualify you to be a spiritual mother to someone. Remember, if you're 20 years old, the 15-year-old is looking up to you!"

When my next-door neighbor Ruth was 15, I was nine and thought of her as an adult. To me, she was a model of Christian womanhood—a sweet, unselfish, friendly, loving Christian girl—the next-door neighbor who paid attention to me.

"How many younger women can we take into our hearts at one time?" I next asked Elisabeth.

As many as God sends! But I don't think we should go rushing around trying to gather together a group. Women sometimes tell me that I am to them what Amy Carmichael was to me, and I think, "Lord, You know that I'm not in that category. I'm not qualified for that." But that's not really my business. I keep going back to the verse where Jesus says, "You didn't choose me. I chose you." So let's be willing to be available, to be broken bread and poured-out wine for as many younger women as God puts in our path.

Interestingly, Elisabeth never met Amy Carmichael, the Irish missionary to South India who founded Dohnavur Fellowship, a refuge for children in danger. She served in India for 53 years and died in 1951 after spending the last 20 years of her life bedridden and in pain. Elisabeth got to know Amy through her books. In the preface of the biography Elisabeth wrote about Amy's life, *A Chance to Die*, Elisabeth notes, "Dohnavur became a familiar place. I knew its bungalows, its paths, its people; I breathed its air. Amy Carmichael became for me what some now call a role model. She was far more than that....She showed me the shape of godliness." Continuing her thoughts on availability, Elisabeth said:

I have to pray that the Lord will enable me to live in such a way as to be an example to people I don't even know. God has given me a public ministry. That word ministry means "servant-hood." A mother has a ministry; a wife has a ministry. You need not have a public platform. You may be ministering to those around you when you least expect it and in very simple ways. We can learn a lot just from watching godly older women who may have no idea of the impact they have on our lives.

With this in mind, I questioned Elisabeth about our relationship. "Do you see me as a Titus 2 'younger woman' in your life?" I asked. She responded:

I wouldn't, Dotto, except that you tell me I am! I have to accept your testimony and the fact that you've told me that you see me as a mentor, spiritual mother, older woman, and I thank God for that privilege.

I wondered whom Elisabeth had learned things from and asked her who had been the most significant older women in her life. She replied:

Of course my mother. She was by far the most significant older woman in my life and the only person who really came to mind as belonging in this category.

The next most important woman who greatly influenced my life was Mrs. DuBose, headmistress of the school I attended in Florida. She was extremely hard on me. She was also gifted with the ability to discern potential in people. So to her I owe a great debt. She saw in me potential I would never have recognized myself, and she forced me to work on those areas. So I learned to play the piano, sing, write, speak on platform, and do things like that in my mid-teens.

Then when I was in college, an older woman was both my housemother and Sunday school teacher—Miss Cumming. She was also among the most influential. It is, however, only in retrospect that I look back and see that God, in His mercy and love, gave me a number of older women who greatly influenced my life.

A Titus 2 Ministry Today

Thinking about the state of our society and the direction it's headed, I then asked Elisabeth about the role of the older women in today's culture. Will the Titus 2 woman become even more valuable during the next 20 years?

> Yes! I certainly think that when people don't have a Christian mother or have a mother who is not living as a Christian mother should, there is a great need for others to pick up that responsibility. That's why it's important that we lodge in the minds of all Christian women that they are meant to be mothers not necessarily in the biological sense but always in the spiritual sense.
>
> We grandmothers have all this great wisdom and all this experience (she says tongue-in-cheek), "What are we supposed to do with it?" But a serious and more important question is, "What does God want us to do with the information we have?"

I had a conversation with a woman who said, "I'm an available woman." I liked that term, so I said, "What do you mean by that?" She replied, "I am available when people need me. I have time to read my Bible, time to pray, time to counsel with other people."

The retirement years present us with serious temptations—to idleness, to self-indulgence, to pampering. This is a colossal waste of God-given gifts. God has given wisdom, strength, experience—and He is giving us the gift of old age. Do we think of it as a gift? These are called "the golden years," yet so many people deplore them, dread them, deny them, insisting that they are not old. Joseph Addison's hymn says, "Through every period of my life Thy goodness I'll pursue," and that is one of my prayers for myself. It is also the prayer of the psalmist who prayed, "Teach us to number our days, that we may apply our hearts unto wisdom" (Psalm 90:12 KJV).

Hearing Elisabeth's comments, I couldn't help wondering why older women aren't seeking out younger women more today. Maybe the following poem by an anonymous author is right!

The Grandmother's Poem

In the dim and distant past
When life's tempo wasn't fast
Gramma used to rock and knit,
Crochet and tat, and babysit.

Gramma now is at the gym
Exercising to keep slim.
Now she's golfing with the bunch,
Taking clients out to lunch,

> *Going north to ski and curl,*
> *And all her days are in a whirl.*
> *Nothing seems to stop or block her*
> *Now that Gramma's off her rocker.*

Why is there sometimes a striking difference between the older women we meet in books (in the Bible or in other accounts of great Christian women who have gone before us) and the older women we meet in real life? I asked Elisabeth, "Isn't the living out the life of Christ what the older woman–younger woman relationship is all about?"

> I think each individual is meant to walk before God in such a way that the life of Christ in her mortal flesh is visible. In Titus 2, Paul is not talking about writing books, giving lectures, and holding Bible classes. He is saying, "Teach," which means "to show." It's "show and tell," and it's more showing than it is telling. Everyone knows that what we are is far more influential and powerful than anything we ever say. But if we have things to say, then people have a right to look for evidence that we live by our words.

But do other older women often feel inadequate and even afraid to respond to God's call to them in Titus 2?

> If we are going to do something for God, we first need to acknowledge our weakness and our inadequacy. Practically everybody in the Bible who ever did anything for God had an argument with Him—"You picked the wrong man, the wrong tribe. What am I going to do? Nobody is going to listen to me." There's Jeremiah, Gideon, David, Moses. Mary didn't

quarrel with God, but she did ask, "How can this be?" and was overwhelmed by the tremendous gift that was being given to her. Then, of course, she was humble enough just to receive it and be thankful.

Nothing is going to make us more soberly aware of our inadequacy than spiritual responsibility. But let us not excuse ourselves. As Moses was saying, "Who am I?" God was saying, "It doesn't matter who you are. I AM is sending you."

If anyone thinks she's qualified and would make a great spiritual mentor, then I'd say she's not qualified!

Each of us should be directed primarily toward God—doing what He says, living the way He describes the Christian life, and trusting that God, in His own way, in His sovereign plan and working in our lives, will bring the older woman and younger woman into contact with each other when He sees the need for that. Daily we should be saying to Him, "I'm yours, Lord. Show me what I can do for You today."

The Bible's "Older Woman"

Knowing the importance of the Titus teaching for relationships between women of God, I was curious and asked Elisabeth what other passages of Scripture support— if not command—this special ministry:

Psalm 145:4 builds on this Titus 2 concept— "One generation shall praise Thy works to another, and shall declare Thy mighty acts."

First Timothy 5 talks about helping the widows. That description of widows is what any Christian woman was expected to have been doing all her life.

Elisabeth makes a good point. In 1 Timothy 5:3-10, we read about older Christian women who have practiced piety in regard to their own family, fixed their hope on God, prayed day and night, lived above reproach, earned a reputation for good works, showed hospitality to strangers, washed the saints' feet, helped those in distress, and devoted themselves to good works. These women certainly sound like good candidates for a Titus 2 ministry to younger women!

The Word Made Flesh

Some concepts covered by Scripture are rather abstract. I asked Elisabeth if there weren't some things that can only be taught by passing them on, one woman of God to another.

> You are talking about the great principle of the Word made flesh, and it certainly is true that the word of Christ has to be made flesh in each of us. At the same time, the flesh has to become the word. When a woman is in love, for instance, she not only wants the presence of her lover, but she wants his word, too. She wants him to write a note with a rose that says, "I love you." She wants to hear him say, "I love you." So flesh has to become word and word has to become flesh. That is the truth of Scripture. And that—God's Word that has become flesh and flesh that has become word—is what women are looking for.

Amen and amen! And thank you, Elisabeth!

30-Week Mentoring Guide

～

*T*he material in this "study guide" was developed as a 30-week approach for an older woman/younger woman mentoring relationship. You'll find practical tips for developing a stronger, more vibrant relationship with the Lord, building a solid marriage, raising well-adjusted children.

I have attempted to keep the information simple and succinct so that you are able to add your life imprint to each session. Your willingness to pass your life perspective to a younger woman can change the course of her life. As you do so, don't hold back from sharing your own failures or times of desperation as well as the times in your life that have been filled with celebration.

It is my prayer that God will use this material to encourage you and your daughter-of-the-heart and take you both on to maturity in Christ!

Meeting 1
The Character of a Christian

Plan, Prepare, and Pray

Each week, remember to confirm with your young friend the time and location of your session together. Remember, too, that every time you have contact you will encourage her. For starters, you might suggest that she read **Psalm 15**, the "Christian Constitution."

Read and meditate on **Psalm 15**. This would be a perfect lesson to use your dictionary and write down the multiple definitions for the word "character." In addition, if you have any books of famous quotes, you might like to use a few of them for your session. Here is one by Oswald Chambers to start with: "My worth to God in public is what I am in private."

Prayer

Lord, help me see the difference between being a Christian and having character. As a woman who desires to please God, may I be willing to forego the easy side of the street and step onto higher ground where standing tall for Christ is demanded.

Share Together

Ask your young friend to describe in her own words her concept of character.

In a society where individual rights have reached gargantuan proportions, to be a woman with character means understanding your role as a servant.

Becoming a Christian does not automatically give you character any more than living in a garage would make you a car. Character is a tool to keep you from falling into the traps of the enemy, and the power behind that tool is your faith in Jesus.

Consider the difference between character and reputation. Abraham Lincoln said, "Character is like a tree and reputation like its shadow. The shadow is what we think of it, the tree is the real thing." Here is an easy way to remember the difference:

- Reputation is who people think you are.

- Character is who you really are.

Only you and God know the difference.

Let's Talk About It

1. When you were a child, was character an important issue in your home?

2. Does character impact your work? Would you hire an extremely qualified employee who had less than a sterling character?

3. Does it take courage to have character? Does it take discipline? Explain your answers.

4. In your opinion, does it take suffering and pain to build character in a person?

5. Share about a time when you were affected by someone's reputation.

Pray for Each Other

As you join hands and pray together today, ask God to show you areas in your character that need refining. Be willing to take the steps necessary to participate in God's plan for improving your character.

Grow Together

Decide if you want to make a commitment to attempt to change during the time between now and your next session. If you do, make sure the area is addressed clearly. Consider reading Psalm 15 daily until you meet again.

∽ Mentoring Moment ∽

"Character is what you are in the dark."
—DWIGHT L. MOODY

Taming the Tongue

Plan, Prepare, and Pray

Suggest that your young friend read some or all of the Scripture verses below. This is a transforming topic, and there are scores of relevant passages in addition to the ones listed. If time permits, offer more verses.

Read *Job 19:2; Psalm 19:2,3; Ephesians 4:25; Colossians 3:9; Proverbs 5:3,4; 16:27; 26:7; 29:20; Ecclesiastes 3:7; 2 Timothy 2:16;* and *James 3:5-12.* Review in your mind and heart any sermons, books, or quotes on the topic of the tongue, gossip, or talking. This issue is a challenge for everyone, so be prepared to dig in and discover how it has influenced your young partner. Be prepared to talk about words and the tone of your voice. Words are a product of the condition of our hearts, and the tongue controls the entire body. Discuss those you talk to daily: children, Jesus, phone callers, mates, and so on.

Prayer

Dear Jesus, it is impossible to tame my tongue apart from Your power. I acknowledge the difficulty I have experienced because I did not keep a guard over my mouth. Please help me assist this young woman in understanding how to control her words.

Share Together

Begin by finding out what words have been spoken to your friend that she holds in her heart. Were they hurtful? Helpful? Who spoke them? When?

The key concepts here are telling the truth and listening. When we speak, we must tell others and ourselves the truth. For instance, an abortion is just that—not an end to an unwanted pregnancy. If you are mad, admit you are mad and don't say, "Oh, I am just upset!" When asked to help with a project, be truthful...let your *yes* be your *yes* and your *no* be *no*. Be honest in what you say.

Listening is an art that is more difficult for some to master than for others. Be quick to listen to God and others; be slow to speak. We tend to speak hastily and defensively when God instructs us and we don't want to hear it.

Let's Talk About It

1. Have you struggled with the issue of talking too much? Too little?

2. Do you use silence or chatter to manipulate—to keep someone at a distance or to keep her from talking so you don't have to listen?

3. Is what you say okay, but how you say it needs some work?

4. Does what you say have any connection to what you read, watch, or listen to?

Pray for Each Other

During this session of prayer, make a time for silence. Ask God to remind you of any word spoken against another that needs forgiveness. Following silence and confession, ask God to correct your heart and its hurts so kindness will flow from your lips. Also include a time of listening for God's direction in your lives.

Grow Together

Decide if you want to commit to any specific action regarding the tongue. If so, hold each other accountable to accomplish that commitment while you are apart. Consider memorizing the following 12 verses taken from the New International version, which are only a few of the many that deal with the tongue.

- He who guards his lips guards his life, but he who speaks rashly will come to ruin (Proverbs 13:3).

- Do you see a man who speaks in haste? There is more hope for a fool than for him (Proverbs 29:20).

- He who answers before listening—that is his folly and his shame (Proverbs 18:13).

- But I tell you that men will have to give account on the day of judgment for every careless word they have spoken (Matthew 12:36).

- Do not let any unwholesome talk come out of your mouths, but only what is helpful for building others up according to their needs, that it may benefit those who listen (Ephesians 4:29).

- A man finds joy in giving an apt reply—and how good is a timely word! (Proverbs 15:23).

- He who guards his mouth and his tongue keeps himself from calamity (Proverbs 21:23).

- A gentle answer turns away wrath, but a harsh word stirs up anger....The tongue that brings healing is a tree of life, but a deceitful tongue crushes the spirit (Proverbs 15:1,4).

- Even a fool is thought wise if he keeps silent, and discerning if he holds his tongue (Proverbs 17:28).

- The words of a gossip are like choice morsels; they go down to a man's inmost parts (Proverbs 18:8).

- For "whosoever would love life and see good days must keep his tongue from evil and his lips from deceitful speech" (1 Peter 3:10).

- If anyone considers himself religious and yet does not keep a tight rein on his tongue, he deceives himself and his religion is worthless (James 1:26).

By memorizing these you will be building a "Scriptural guard" to check your words before you say them.

Meeting 3
Reasons to Stay Home

Plan, Prepare, and Pray

Ask your friend to be prepared to discuss her decision about having children and then why she chose to work or stay at home, whichever applies.

Read and meditate on *Titus 2:3-5; Proverbs 31:27,28;* and *Matthew 6:33*. Consider these aspects of a career outside the home: your own preference, the pressure of popular culture, financial needs, and/or the wishes of your husband. (My book, *The Stay-at-Home Mom* is a great resource for exploring this topic.)

This session will provide opportunities to talk about money, including how to make money at home, if necessary, and how to save money. Many statistics confirm the difference in a child's attitudes and actions when he is being raised full-time by his mother at home. Don't hesitate to speak directly.

Prayer

Father God, do I have a bias on this subject? Am I able to assist this young woman in making a decision that would please You? If I made a poor decision as a young mother, have I asked forgiveness? Make me willing to be honest before this young woman.

Share Together

To set the stage for today's topic, ask if your friend's mother was a stay-at-home mom. If so, what does your daughter-of-the-

heart most enjoy or remember about her mother? If not, what was hard about not having her mother available?

Here are three main ideas: 1) Being home full-time encourages your faith to grow; 2) you are the best choice to parent; 3) the facts are in.

When we are home and needing to declare our dependence daily, we see God work. He sends finances and food and everything we need. Our faith grows, and we are able to show our children that God is trustworthy.

Daily you can see the impact of your decision on your children. No one can make decisions and choices for your child as well as you can. Children need their mothers. In 1992 more than 14 million women were home full-time with their children. In 1998, the number had grown to 19 million women staying at home. The facts indicate that children grow to be more productive and useful if a mother's hand guides and directs as the primary caregiver.

Let's Talk About It

1. Have you considered why you want to stay at home or go to work?

2. Are finances the major consideration when you face staying home?

3. Are you able to believe that God has given you the responsibility to raise your children but that they still belong to Him?

4. Do you and your mate agree on the issue of staying at home?

5. If you are a single mother, can you still stay at home?

6. Do you have a hard time experiencing contentment?

Pray for Each Other

Confide in each other about longings of your heart. If you have had an expensive education and a fulfilling career, be grateful for these gifts and offer them to God as tools to raise children for Him.

Grow Together

Decide if you want to commit to any specific act between now and your next session. Example: Each day I will hunt for circumstances through which I see God enlarging my faith. No matter how difficult or easy this topic is for you and your young friend, you will need to encourage her to be steadfast. Raising children is a 20-year investment. The choice to stay at home is sometimes ridiculed. Ask God to grant comfort and assurance in the choice to be a stay-at-home mom.

∼ *Mentoring Moment* ∼

Wet Oatmeal Kisses

The baby is teething. The children are fighting.
Your husband just called and said,
"Eat dinner without me."
One of these days you'll explode and
shout to the kids,
"Why don't you grow up and act your age?"
And they will.

Or, "You guys get outside and find
yourselves something to do.
And don't slam the door!" And they don't.
You'll straighten their bedrooms all neat and tidy,
toys displayed on the shelf hangers

in the closet, animals caged. You'll yell,
"Now I want it to stay this way!" And it will.

You will prepare a perfect dinner with a salad
that hasn't had all the olives picked out
and a cake with no finger traces in the icing and you'll say,
"Now THIS is a meal for company."
And you will eat it alone.

You'll yell, "I want complete privacy on the phone. No
screaming. Do you hear me?"
And no one will answer. No more plastic tablecloths stained
with spaghetti.
No more dandelion bouquets.
No more iron-on patches.
No more wet, knotted shoelaces,
muddy boots or rubber bands for ponytails.

Imagine. A lipstick with a point.
No babysitter for New Year's Eve,
washing clothes only once a week, no PTA meetings or silly
school plays where your
child is a tree. No carpools,
blaring stereos or forgotten lunch money.

No more Christmas presents made of library paste and
toothpicks.
No more wet oatmeal kisses.
No more tooth fairy.
No more giggles in the dark, scraped knees
to kiss or sticky fingers to clean.
Only a voice asking: "Why don't you grow up?"

And the silence echoes: "I did."

—ANONYMOUS

Meeting 4
Disciplines of a Godly Woman

Plan, Prepare, and Pray

Think of this session as one that can head in several directions: a call to Christ, a deeper commitment as a woman of God, or perhaps facing and dealing seriously with sin.

Read and meditate on the following Scriptures: *Romans 12:1,2; John 10:10; 1 Samuel 16:7; Galatians 5:22,23; 2 Corinthians 4:16,17;* and *Romans 9:20,21.* Determine as best you can which direction your young partner most needs to go, and prepare your heart to head in that direction. If you are not certain of her decision for Christ, you may want to have additional material available. I would suggest the Four Spiritual Laws booklet produced by Campus Crusade for Christ. You might also prepare to do a word study on "discipline," and evaluate how our society deals with discipline.

This may be a reality-check session. Often we want to achieve something without the discipline required to do so. If discipline is lacking in one area, usually it is lacking in others as well. Develop this topic and look for ways to help create discipline in your lives.

Prayer

Father, help me return in memory to the day I found You in my heart. Do I still have my "first love"? Help me assist this young woman in seeking Your face. Be the leader in our discussion, and help us both desire to be godly.

Share Together

As suggested earlier, if you are uncertain of your young partner's relationship with Christ, be sure you start this session with an opportunity for her to make Jesus first in her world. Make sure these concepts are understood: acceptance of self as God made her, recognition of God's deep love for her, and acknowledgment that God is good and so is everything He does. From this framework, you can approach any or all of the following:

Bible study	Prayer	Service
Giftedness	Abilities	Attitudes
Being vs. doing	Fruit of the Spirit	God's will

Let's Talk About It

1. What keeps you from consistency in your spiritual growth?

2. Discuss the areas in your life that demonstrate a lack of discipline.

3. Look at the topics listed under "Share Together." Which of these would you begin expending energy on immediately?

4. Is Jesus your first love? Do you sense that He is relegated to a place lower than first place?

5. How does the world squeeze you into its mold for living each day? How would you like to change that?

Pray for Each Other

Now is a great time to make this statement: "I have not arrived...but I am surviving." Seek to be honest in your prayer time. Freely confess the need for more of God in your world. We can never achieve godliness; rather, we become more godly as we draw closer to God. If this session has helped your young friend recognize a need, this prayer time could be a turning point in her life. Don't rush—let the Holy Spirit do His job in both of your hearts.

Grow Together

This lesson really calls for some specific action. Take the time to assess that action and make a commitment to each other. It may be as simple as choosing to show more love to others or as intense as giving up a lifelong habit that separates you from God.

Fashioning Your Mental Wardrobe

Plan, Prepare, and Pray

Read and meditate on *Deuteronomy 6:6-10; Colossians 3:12-17; Psalm 24:4;* and *Psalm 101:3.* You may find it helpful to consult a dictionary for a definition of "purity." Find examples from current magazines, TV shows, and films to demonstrate the difficulty of maintaining a pure life in our society.

Practice answering the question "What will I wear today?" with principles from the Colossians passage listed above. Browse through a fashion magazine and have some fun exploring styles, colors, wardrobe planning, and even closet cleaning! Then consider issues of appropriateness and motivation.

Prayer

Lord, I want to be pure as You are pure. Have I allowed unwholesome actions, images, or thoughts to dwell in me? Help me rely on Your promptings toward holiness as I seek to grow in You.

Share Together

Much like we clothe our bodies, we clothe our minds. What should we put on mentally today? Biblical thinking!

Currently popular "politically correct" thinking allows for no absolutes, focuses solely on the rights of the individual, and scoffs at the idea of dying to self and living for God's glory. These attitudes have even invaded some churches, resulting in Christians who confuse someone's well-meaning agenda with what God actually says.

Lead your young friend to understand the importance of deliberately putting on biblical thinking every hour of every day. No more wondering what to wear!

Let's Talk About It

1. How much time do you spend on your wardrobe? Don't forget to include shopping, washing, ironing, dressing, and experimenting with new looks.

2. Do you spend as much time developing your mental wardrobe? Why or why not?

3. If the concept of "mental dressing" is new to you, give yourself time to absorb and implement this new challenge.

4. Have you developed thought patterns that may need to be revised? If so, search for relevant topics in the Scriptures to gain God's perspective on your thoughts.

5. Consider the important people in your life. How does their thinking affect you? Are you allowing their thoughts to direct yours?

Pray for Each Other

Ask God to help you see your thought patterns as He does to free you from feeling fearful about giving up ways of thinking that have become comfortable over the years. We want to have the mind of Christ and to wear apparel that separates us from the world's thinking.

Grow Together

Consider challenging each other to memorize Colossians 3:12-17 to help you think about your mental wardrobe at least as often as you think about your fashion wardrobe. Ask God to help you avoid being too preoccupied with or not concerned enough about your outer appearance. Seek a balance that will please Him.

Meeting 6
Being Imitators

Plan, Prepare, and Pray

Read and meditate on *1 Thessalonians 1:6,7; 2:14; Hebrews 6:12; 13:7; 2 Thessalonians 3:7; Colossians 3:10; 3 John 11;* and *Ephesians 5:1*. Find a dictionary definition for the word "imitation." Consider the implications of being a follower in relation to the way an actor mimics.

Find examples of famous personalities and performers who are currently being mimicked. Perhaps it's a hairstyle, a fitness program, or an attitude that is being copied across the country. Remember when hula hoops were all the rage? Remember when one commercial sparked the popular rude response, "Not!"?

Prayer

Father, please show me the people and things I have tended to imitate in the past. Have I felt compelled to follow the crowd? Whom do I desire to imitate now?

Share Together

Play a round of "Simon Says" to set the tone for a discussion on what it means to be a follower. Try to remember incidents from childhood or adolescence when you and your friends played "Simon Says" in real life.

Sometimes we are drawn to imitate a public figure for the wrong reasons. We find ourselves attracted by wealth, beauty, popularity, or personality, often overlooking more worthwhile qualities in someone who may be far from the spotlight. Before you follow someone's example, check out his or her values. The next best thing to being wise is to live in a circle of those who are.

Let's Talk About It

1. What does it mean to be a follower?

2. Upon reflection, did you discover that you have been imitating someone without realizing it? Who and why?

3. When choosing someone to follow, should character or performance be the primary consideration?

4. What does the Bible say about being "followers of Christ"?

5. Can you see why it is less desirable to follow a person than to follow the Christ you see in that person? Explain.

Pray for Each Other

Ask God to reveal areas where you may be following unwisely. Make a commitment to seek God and people who honor Him. Ask Him to provide wisdom to discern positive mentors for you to imitate.

Grow Together

Be sure to encourage your friend to reevaluate the relationships in her world. She may need extra help if she has just recognized the dangers of an unhealthy relationship or unwise imitation. Pray together. If the situation allows, you will find it meaningful to kneel together in humility before God while seeking sensitivity in the area of relationships that need to be changed. Let God direct your efforts for His holy purposes.

Meeting 7
Unity

Plan, Prepare, and Pray

Meditate on the *book of Ephesians, especially chapter 4:1-6*. Think about the concept of unity in your world.

Find a book or a magazine on gardening, or make a trip to the nursery near your home. Do your best to discover the concept of unity in the gardening field.

Prayer

Lord, help me see the reasons why I am not unified with You and with Your family. If unforgiveness stands in the way of my being in unity with You, I desire to confess my sins and to be made right and whole.

Share Together

Look up the word "unified" in the dictionary together. Allow your daughter-of-the-heart to brainstorm her ideas and concepts about this very important topic as a member of the family of God.

I am a gardener of sorts. I grow both flowers and vegetables. Living in the sunny, warm, arid state of Arizona, the opportunity to garden most of the year is available to me. My experiences in gardening have brought me closer to understanding how, just like the sun, water, and plants in my gardens, believers are to work together.

In the book of Ephesians, Paul encourages the church to love one another. He uses the word "love" 9 times in 6 chapters in this book, while he uses the word only 23 in all of the other letters he writes. He tells his readers that there are no differences in Christ; there are not Jews and Gentiles, just fellow men and women in Christ. Seven elements of unity are found in Ephesians 4:4-6. They are:

1. One body—the church of Jesus

2. One Spirit—the Holy Spirit

3. One hope—the future, which is the same for all of us

4. One Lord—the head of the church

5. One faith—the subjective faith which we exercise

6. One baptism—water or not, it refers to our identification with Christ

7. One God and Father—the relationship God has with all of us

We are planted together and growing together—experiencing Christ and increasing our understanding of who we are in Him. We are one, not many. When I plant vegetables, they are vegetables—a variety of plants in one garden, with one gardener, one sun, and one water source. It's the same with mixed flower seeds. They are a combination of flowers in one package needing the gardener, water, and sun to help them grow.

We are united by the act of the cross. Those outside the family of God are able to see the work of the cross in our lives by the unity we live. It's important for us to stay connected to Jesus and to one another at all costs. Differences are expected. They make us interesting to talk to, but they should never separate us.

Let's Talk About It

1. Do you regularly find discord with certain individuals or certain personality types? If so, why?

2. As a child did you see unity lived out in your family? In your church?

3. What is the closest group of people you have ever been a part of? What made it so close?

4. What does it take for you to personally feel a sense of unity with other believers?

5. Describe a time when you were left out.

Pray for Each Other

As you pray together, hold hands and draw as close to one another as possible for a sense of unity. This prayer time would be a good time to ask one another the question, "Are we okay with each other?" If not, you can talk it out together. If all is well, you can thank God for the unity you share and enjoy.

Grow Together

This week agree to evaluate relationships each of you have with family and friends. Are these relationships demonstrating unity?

Meeting 8
Knowing and Finding His Purpose

Plan, Prepare, and Pray

Before your next meeting, call your young friend and ask her to be prepared to share a decision she has made. In the process of this decision, what tools did she use to find God's will?

Read *Matthew 21:37-30; Acts 5:29; Colossians 3; 4:2-4; Titus 2:3-5; Hebrews 11:8;* and *1 Peter 1:2.* Meditate on these passages as well as others that provide you with instructions and with God's desire for obedience in our lives.

We all make decisions on a daily basis. Each decision influences us much more than we may imagine. Consider the following daily decisions and their ramifications:

- The time you get up

- What you eat

- The way you drive to work

- How you speak to your family and friends

- How you spend your time

Prayer

Lord, I have seen Your purpose and will in my life through carefully studying and following Your Word. The way of God is the direction found in the Scriptures. May I find the words to encourage my daughter-of-the-heart to seek Your will and obey it daily.

Share Together

As you begin your time together, ask her the questions you asked and answered this week. Review the simple, practical decisions you make daily, and use these points as a place to jump into the discussion on finding and knowing God's will.

Every day Christians ask, "What is God's will for my life?" The question is often followed by, "How do I find God's will?" or "How do I know if it is God's will?"

Perhaps you are like me. I'd like Jesus to write me a book of my own, and each chapter would represent a decade of my life, and each paragraph would tell me how to live each year within decade. The reality is that there are no books named Donna in the Bible, but they all have my name written in them.

To know His will is to know Him. To study His Word and His commands is to know Him. If you are already. . .

- Committed to Christ as Lord of your life

- Reading His Word

- Listening to His Holy Spirit

- Praying

- Witnessing

- Fellowshipping with other believers

- Knowing and using your spiritual gifts

- Studying His Word

- Meditating

- Serving others

...then your ability to know Him and listen to Him is already in place. When you make a decision, you know the Word well enough to know that whatever you are deciding is not in conflict with His instructions. Each portion of your decision is found in knowing God. If you know God, you will know His will.

Elisabeth Elliot reduces making decisions and knowing God's will to the ability to trust and obey. If you know, you can trust. If you trust, you will obey.

Let's Talk About It

1. What was the hardest decision you ever made? Why?

2. What was the best decision you made? Why? How did you make that choice?

3. Reflect and discuss a time when you made a bad decision. Talk through the process, the decision, and the results.

4. What, regarding God's will in your life, are you certain about?

5. List three specific things that you are certain are God's will. Example: It is God's will that all people should know Him.

Pray for Each Other

Make the time, as well as the prayer, a time of unraveling what you know about God and His Word. We can accept information as truth and discover later it is not truth. Ask God to reveal any pieces of information that may not be truth.

Grow Together

Ask your young friend if she has a decision pending for which she is searching for God's answer and direction. If so, use this as a teaching tool to help her align her thinking with God's. Pray over each of the topics you have discussed today.

Meeting 9
Busyness

Plan, Prepare, and Pray

Call your young friend and ask her to consider areas of her life where she feels too busy and be prepared to talk about those areas. Additionally, ask her to keep a log of her activities for the next seven days. (You may want to provide her a prepared sheet that will allow her to just fill in the blanks.)

Make a log of your own week. Decide what you would like to adjust. Anne Ortlund encourages women to reevaluate their schedules regularly—every five years—to take a serious look at not only activities and priorities, but also belief systems. This helps you know where you spend your time and how you to spend your time. Then you can begin to adjust your life if it's not balanced.

If you have these books, scan their information: *Get More Done in Less Time* by Donna Otto; *Tyranny of the Urgent* by Charles Hummel; *Ordering Your Private World* by Gordon McDonald; *Discipline, the Glad Surrender* by Elisabeth Elliot; *Celebration of Discipline* (chapter on solitude) by Richard Foster.

Prayer

Dear Jesus, help me clear my thoughts and rearrange my own priorities, allowing me to see how I use my time. Also give me the ability to see why I hurry, hurry, hurry. Finally, help me be willing to rearrange my life to make it less busy.

Share Together

Begin your session by going over your daily log for the past week. If either one of you did not do a log, discuss why. If "you were too busy," recall, in one-hour increments, how you spent each day.

A friend sent me a "Cathy" card (by Cathy Guisewite) that said, "I'm too busy to call. I'm too busy to visit. I'm too busy to write a letter." As you open the card you see Cathy with her best grin standing in front of a greeting card display case. She is holding a few cards and has more at her feet. The caption reads, "However, I've managed to find seven hours to stand around reading all the greeting cards." The humor of the card is outweighed by the ring of truth. We always have time to do what we want to do. How does this busyness creep into our lives? Here are a few possibilities:

- We think busyness is good or godly.

- Busyness makes us look important.

- Busyness makes us feel important.

- Modern conveniences give us more time.

- We can't decide.

- We say yes more than no, or just don't know when to say which.

- Busyness is progress.

- Everyone is busy, so just "buck up."

- Our culture is busy, and we must keep up.

To counteract this way of busyness we must make time for solitude and restoration. Taking time for quiet is essential if we are to hear from God about the direction of our lives. If we're too busy to pray and find quiet before the God of the Universe—the Lord of our lives—we are TOO busy.

Let's Talk About It

1. Do you say "hurry up" to your children? How often?

2. Do you exceed the speed limit to get places on time? How often?

3. Is dinner hour just a few minutes? Do you eat in the car?

4. Does your life have quiet time? How often? By accident or by schedule?

5. Describe how you feel when you are rushing, rushing, rushing.

Pray for Each Other

Take time today for a longer session of prayer. Help each other quiet your hearts and minds long enough to sense rest and peacefulness. Be willing to heed what you hear from this time of prayer and quiet. Perhaps you could change your location for this time of prayer. If there is a garden near your meeting location, you might consider going there.

Grow Together

The possibilities for accountability and assistance to one another as a result of this session are many. Consider these suggestions:

- Rise early and phone each other one day this week.

- If your young friend has children, offer to watch the children while she has a quiet session.

- Perhaps an extra time together just for more prayer and quiet could be worked into your schedule.

- Hold each other accountable for a ten-minute-per-day time of solitude.

- Encourage each other to cut out or slow down in one area of your lives.

- Use your imagination about other ways to cut back on busyness.

Trying Trust

Plan, Prepare, and Pray

Suggest to your friend that she read the *first two chapters of Job* this week. You can read as much of the book of Job as possible, but especially the first two chapters and **13:15**. Trust can be linked to adversity or prosperity. Job trusted through times of prosperity and adversity. His life is a great model for us. Make a list of ways we choose to trust people. Take time with this list. You will be amazed how many times we choose to trust others in our day-to-day activities. For example, we trust the Department of Transportation as it establishes the stop signs, red lights, and speed limits in our cities.

Prayer

Lord, help me to understand this concept of trust in a deep way. I desire to trust You in all things, not just in the situations I choose. May I understand Your sufficiency and trust You more.

Share Together

Go over your list of "trusts" with your young friend. Give her opportunities to add to your list. This will set the stage for acknowledging the ability to trust and move closer to trusting as Job did.

The amazing story of the life of Job is very powerful. Job is one of the oldest (perhaps the oldest) and longest books of the Bible. Many scholars believe it was likely written by Job. While many find the story sad or discouraging, I find it very stimulating. Job has grown and seems to fully understand and live out the New Testament principle of "I am the vine; you are the branches. If a man remains in me and I in him, he will bear much fruit; apart from me you can do nothing" (John 15:5).

While this book has 42 chapters, like a good author, the writer gets right to the heart of the message by describing Job three different ways in the first 25 verses. He is "blameless, upright and fearing God." Job writes nine of the most powerful words ever written: "Though he slay me, yet will I hope [trust] in him."

Job's character is blameless. He acknowledges that all of his belongings come from God and belong to God. Job attests that he came naked into the world and will leave the same, proudly proclaiming that apart from God he is nothing.

Suddenly this wealthy, prominent man is attacked. Satan attacks with God's permission. The attacks have only one boundary—Satan can take family, health, and possessions, but not Job's life. Yet after being attacked on all of these fronts, Job still trusts. He understands two significant traits of trust: 1) God, the object of his trust, is trustworthy; 2) Trust is a choice.

Let's Talk About It

1. Discuss the attributes of God.

2. Try to discover why trusting is personally hard. Often life experiences sabotage our trust levels.

3. Who do you trust most on this earth? Why?

4. What would you be able to lay down before God to demonstrate your trust?

Pray for Each Other

Trust is essential to our walk of faith. To allow God to be the Lord of our lives and submit all to Him is not easy, but it is what God desires from us, and He has enabled us to accomplish this as we walk on earth.

Grow Together

As you leave one another, select one specific area in your lives to trust in the Lord until you meet again. You may want to memorize Proverbs 3:5,6: "Trust in the Lord with all your heart and lean not on your own understanding; in all your ways acknowledge him, and he will make your paths straight."

Meeting 11
"At-One-Ment"

Plan, Prepare, and Pray

Read *Exodus 20; Luke 3:14; 2 Corinthians 12:10; Philippians 4:11; 1 Timothy 6:6-8;* and *Hebrews 13:5.* We all need reminders and reinforcements about contentment. Meditate on these passages, as well as the book of Acts. If you have a copy of *Foxe's Book of Martyrs,* or any biography of a missionary, reread portions to refresh your memory regarding the sacrifices and determination of the early church.

Most Americans watch TV and read some newspapers or weekly periodicals. Take any one of those and make a list of what you are encouraged to own. In the course of a one-hour TV program or an evening of TV watching, make a list of how many items the merchants try to sell you. Do the same with a magazine. It might be more interesting if you choose a magazine or TV show that is familiar to your young friend. Another idea is to get a small camping tent and set it up as a visual before your daughter-of-the-heart arrives or perhaps you might choose to set it up together. Ask her if she is content (tent). I have done this, and it is very memorable.

Prayer

Jesus, looking around I often see something I want or need. I desire to live in the world, but not be of the world. May I rejoice with those who have more than me. I desire to be content with what Your hand has given me.

Share Together

Take your research from the TV or magazine and examine it together. Discuss how often we are subjected to bigger and better options. This would be a great time to share any personal insight you have regarding your own lack of contentment.

Paul's discussion of contentment found in Philippians sets the stage for today's time together. The apostle instructs us to be content regardles of whether we have much or little. We should work at being well-tented, content in what we have.

This concept of contentment seems simple enough, and I suppose it is clear. The difficulty is working it into our lives. Humans were made to enjoy what we see, and our sin nature causes us to lust. To be satisfied, or to find sufficiency in where we live, how much we eat, what we drive, what we wear, where we go, who our friends are, what our church is, how much education we have, who our children, mates, and parents are, is not a simple task. Hebrews advises us to be content with such things as we have.

Going back to the Ten Commandments, we find that we should not covet our neighbor's home, spouse, male or female servant (dishwasher or bread maker), ox or donkey (new car), anything. The list seems complete. It seems the question is: How do I get from not coveting to contentment?

The answer is through "at-one-ment" with God. Acknowledge His abundance and ability to provide anything and everything. To be content is to be at-one with God and His decisions for your life, to trust Him for all His gifts and goodness to you. He has given you life and all the necessary accessories. Accepting God's plan in our lives is at the root of contentment and satisfaction. While it is true that God ordained that we participate with Him on our journey through life, He did not plan for us to be in charge. That is His task. When I start to covet something, anything, I have allowed myself to become my own god. When I do that, I break yet another of the Ten Commandments: "Thou shalt have no other God before me." It takes trust and practice to be content and at one with God.

Let's Talk About It

1. Do you find yourself comparing what you have and who you are with your friends and family members?

2. Do you think you are ambitious? If so, how could ambition cause you to be discontent?

3. Make a list of the things that cause you temptation.

4. Describe a time when you were grateful and glad for something or for an event that happened in your life.

5. Is contentment an issue in your world? How does it rank with other issues?

Pray for Each Other

Join hands and pray for one another. Seek to be sensitive to what you have already discussed in this session as you ask for God's enablement to move you further into at-onement with Him. The ability to be content and satisfied with God's sufficiency is life-changing.

Grow Together

This is an excellent session to set up some accountability with one another. Perhaps one of you reads too many catalogs, which causes dissatisfaction with what you own, or watches too many romance movies, which can cause dissatisfaction in marriage. After you have explored these areas, set up some kind of checks and balances.

Serving

Plan, Prepare, and Pray

Read *Exodus 24:13; 33:11* and *Matthew 22:37-40; 25:21.*
This lesson should bring you closer to the definition of the
terms "servant," "slave," and "ministry." As you search the
passages listed above, you will also face the issue of how
much love you and your young friend truly have for
mankind. Read the Bible, looking for as many servants of
God and man as you can find.

Serving is not a popular topic. It might be useful to have
some information about the need for volunteers in
America. You might consider calling your local public
school to find how many willing servants are in the class-
rooms. Gather data to illustrate how uncommon it is to find
slaves or servants in the last decade of the twentieth century.

Prayer

*Lord, help me to assess in my own life how willing
I am to serve anyone. May I be honest about the
areas I am willing to give my time and attention to.
As I evaluate these issues in my life, help me to
bring fresh light into the heart of my young friend
about her desire to serve, her need to serve, and the
direction she should take.*

Share Together

As you begin your time together, ask your daughter-of-the-
heart two questions:

1. As best as she can remember, except for her parents, who has served her the most?

2. What is she currently doing that she would call service?

As women committed to making Christ Lord of our lives, serving is important. Once our decision for God is completed, our lives are not our own, and we begin to look for ways to please God. One way we do this is by sharing our faith with others.

We also receive spiritual gifts at the time of our conversion; these gifts belong to the family of God. Each believer has the joy of stewarding these gifts. Add to the spiritual gifts our natural talents and resources of time, energy, and finances, and you begin to see a plan of how we can best serve God and the family of God.

As we mature in our walk with God, we take on the fruit of knowing God in more intimate ways, and growth appears in such areas as kindness, humility, compassion, perseverance, and obedience. Often we begin to find specific opportunities to serve that challenge us.

Joshua was first a servant to Moses; it was actually his official title. (Later he became known as the servant of Jehovah.) Joshua handled many of the details for Moses. The Hebrew word used about Joshua in Exodus is very much like the Greek word that means "deacon." So Joshua served Moses as his deacon. Joshua loved Moses and God, and he learned about serving God by serving Moses. The lawyer in Matthew who asked what the greatest commandment was quickly found that loving God and another were the two on which everything else is based. If I love, I will serve.

My pastor has said for years, "We all want to be slaves/ servants until someone treats us like one."

Let's Talk About It

1. How do you feel about being a servant?

2. As a child did you have regular opportunities to serve family, friends, and neighbors?

3. Do you see the servant as a strong individual or a weak individual?

4. What are your talents, spiritual gifts, and interests?

5. How could you use your talents, spiritual gifts, and interests to serve others?

Pray for Each Other

As you join in prayer over this tremendously important topic, look for ways to serve your young friend. Ask God to reveal anything that hinders the ability to love one another, and give yourself freely to serving one another.

Grow Together

Discuss the possibility of serving together in some work of the Kingdom. Encourage your friend to move forward. If, until now, she has never understood the need to serve one another by loving and looking for ways to minister, affirm her interest and invest in her desire to add serving to her life.

Meeting 13

How to Love Your Husband

Plan, Prepare, and Pray

Find every version you can of the famous passage on love from *1 Corinthians 13*. Read each one, noting phrases and words that quicken your heart. In this session you will dig into God's definition of love as opposed to your own or what you read in magazines. While other sessions will look at tangibles, this lesson is designed to awaken your heart afresh with the delights of this chapter on love.

This is a time to discuss how the concept of love is often misunderstood. Go to what is familiar for examples. Use your dictionary or women's periodicals to demonstrate how differently God sees and teaches love from the way the heart of man perceives it.

Prayer

Dearest loving Lord, do I love? Do I seek to clear my heart from frantic self-seeking long enough to express love for You and for the man You sent me to love? May I truly examine my shortcomings in the light of my many blessings.

Share Together

The writer of 1 Corinthians is Paul. Like me, Paul was a black-and-white kind of person. He was either in or he was out. At first, Paul was dedicated to killing Christians; then, following his acceptance of Jesus, Paul loved Christians and devoted his life to spreading the Christian faith. Paul's background equipped him to understand and communicate love in a very effective way.

If you were to reduce the Ten Commandments to one word, that word would be love. If you love, you will not commit murder or adultery or take God's name in vain. You will honor parents and remember to keep the Sabbath holy.

The key characteristics of love described by Paul are patience, kindness, gentleness, humility, courtesy, selflessness, good disposition, guilelessness, and sincerity. Look for these concepts in 1 Corinthians 13.

Let's Talk About It

1. Did you feel loved as a child? What made you feel loved?

2. Have you accepted notions about love you now see as out of alignment with God's plan? If so, what are they?

3. Which of the key characteristics of love mentioned are the most difficult for you to express? Why?

4. Do you have a choice in love? What is that choice?

5. Take a few minutes to describe a time when you gave and received love with the depth and sincerity we find in this chapter.

Pray for Each Other

Use the answers from questions 2 and 5 to set the tone for your prayer.

Grow Together

Decide if you want to commit to loving your husband in a particular way between now and your next time together.

Example: In response to the chapter on love, I will seek to be more kind to my husband. You may want to memorize a portion of Scripture that will help you in this area. Remember that true love comes out of the heart, and it is the Word hidden in your heart that can give you a new perspective and true love.

Meeting 14
The Way to Your Husband's Heart

Plan, Prepare, and Pray

Read **Romans 15:7; Ephesians 4:32; Psalm 24:3,4; and Romans 12:18.** Refer to "How to Love Your Husband" (Meeting 13). Review your husband's favorite recipes and menus.

Read and meditate on the above Scriptures. Plan your husband's favorite dinner and add more of his favorite foods to next week's marketing list: popsicles, corn chips, canned peaches, ingredients for homemade cookies, or old-fashioned hot dogs like he gets at his favorite sports arena.

This would be a good session to teach your young friend some things about food: its preparation, presentation, and effects on people in our homes. Talk about fragrance or lighting or anything you do to create a special atmosphere for your loved ones.

Prayer

Father, do I find joy in serving the foods my husband likes? Do I think more often about ministering to his needs or manipulating him to meet my needs? Is there really acceptance in my heart for this man you sent to me, or is there just action without acceptance? Help me this week to speak straight from my heart about my relationship with my husband.

Share Together

Having an attitude of acceptance toward your husband's preferences helps you keep short accounts with him.

Be constantly aware of any need to offer and receive forgiveness. If a man is unable or unwilling to ask for forgiveness, then remember to be at peace with him as much as is possible (see Romans 12:18). You will be rewarded by the Father with a peaceful heart for accepting this husband God has given. In time you will be rewarded by your husband in his own way for favoring and serving him. This is not to say you will always be able to serve your husband's favorite meal at the time he prefers and in a perfect atmosphere. But the ability to serve without resentment or pressure is a great gift to marriage.

Let's Talk About It

1. Do you understand "acceptance" as God describes it? Do you acknowledge that people grow in places they feel accepted?

2. Describe a time when you offered an attitude of acceptance and saw someone soften and respond. (Maybe it was you!)

3. Do you seek to minister to your husband? Do you look for his favorites? In what categories besides food can you please him?

4. Write down your husband's two favorite dinners. When was the last time you served them?

5. Take time to discuss how seeking the way to your husband's heart could affect your entire household.

Pray for Each Other

This session may reveal how much hostility can build toward a husband who seeks his own way and does not consider his wife's need or desire for acceptance and for someone to please her with her favorites things. A time of confession may be in order, allowing the Holy Spirit to dig to the bottom of this pain. This may be an excellent time to kneel together in humility, searching the attitude of your hearts toward serving a husband who takes advantage, or it may be a time to praise God for one who lovingly serves back.

Grow Together

Decide together if you want to commit to any specific response between now and your next session. (One gal told me she wanted to cook three meals per week. For her that was a huge step from fast foods and canned soup!)

Meeting 15
Building Your Mate in Love

Plan, Prepare, and Pray

Read and meditate on *Genesis 2:15-25; 1 Corinthians 11:8,9;* and *1 John 4:18.* This session explores ways to build your husband in love. Other sessions on marriage address offering acceptance, being submissive, honoring his favorites, and communicating. But in this time together, simply look for ways to build up your husband—God's ways, not yours!

Make a list of some basic building blocks to help your young partner. Don't be too shy to add appropriate intimate tools. Refer to the building of a marriage in terms of construction: Jesus is the foundation, the husband is the center beam.

Prayer

Father, what are some of the ways You have directed me to build up my husband? Please give me some fresh, ideas and perspectives on ways to do this. Help me recognize the times I have torn him down in a selfish attempt to meet my own needs. May I once again be willing to share authentically.

Share Together

Love—pure love, God's love—does cast out fear. Our husbands can be fearful. It is a huge task to take on a wife, children, and home, not to mention a job that requires the biggest bulk of his energy. Demonstrate your pure love so that his fears are assuaged. Offer hope. Listen to his words and his heart.

Watch his body language—look for clues. Speak of the past and future as he gives opportunities, but don't press him to focus on either one. Believe in him. Let him make mistakes without saying "I told you so." Speak words that lift up, not words that tear down. Offer a place of respite.

In the middle of life's storms, hold on tight, get wet, take gulps, and keep holding on until the Storm Calmer, sweet Jesus, calms the waves.

Let's Talk About It

1. Are you certain of God's perfect love? Does it cast out your fears? Describe a specific time when this precious gift was very clear to you.

2. Do you tend to think that only weak people experience fear?

3. Do you acknowledge that fear is a part of your husband's life? Can you recognize the signs?

4. The storm incident as told in the Gospels shows that God has given Jesus authority to calm the seas. Do you see God using you as a suitable helpmate to calm your husband's seas?

5. List five ways you see your husband as the center beam in your world.

Pray for Each Other

"Lord, I give up all my own plans and purposes, all my own desires and hopes, and accept Thy will for my life. I give myself, my life, my all utterly to Thee to be

Thine forever. Fill me and seal me with Thy Holy Spirit. Use me as Thou wilt, send me where Thou wilt, work out Thy whole will in my life at any cost now and forever."

—PRAYER BY BETTY SCOTT STAM

Grow Together

Decide if you want to hold each other accountable to perform a specific deed for the purpose of each of you building up your husbands in love.

∾ *Mentoring Moment* ∾

10 Ways to Build-Up Your Husband

1. *Prepare his breakfast.*

2. *Send him off with a hug and a wave in the morning.*

3. *Stop him and pray for him as he heads for an important meeting.*

4. *Send a treasure in his suitcase, attaché case, or lunch box.*

5. *Write a simple letter and mail it to him.*

6. *Tell him you are going to oil his feet, scratch his back, give him a massage, or whatever calms him, and then do it as planned.*

7. *Listen to him without interrupting.*

8. *Call him at his place of work just to say, "I care about you" or, "I am praying for you."*

9. *Wrap up his favorite snack and put it in his truck or car as he heads to a sporting event.*

10. *Carry his favorite gum, hard candy, or candy bar in your purse when you are going to be together.*

Communicating with Your Mate

Plan, Prepare, and Pray

Marriage topics generate lots of interest. Assign the verses below and ask your friend if she would make a list of the trouble spots that she thinks can threaten communication in a marriage.

Read and meditate on *Proverbs 14:1; Ephesians 5:33; Philippians 2:3,4,14; Mark 10:7-9;* and *1 Corinthians 11:11.* Many fine books have been written on the subject of marriage, and I suggest you refer to any you have on your bookshelves. If you're looking for new material, try any of these (listed in Supplemental Reading List at the end of this book): *Fit to Be Tied; His Needs, Her Needs; The Language of Love;* and *The Marriage Builder.* This is a huge topic, so don't be disappointed if you don't finish. Communication is never done!

Ask your church leaders if they have any quizzes that evaluate communication skills. If not, maybe your local or library or bookstore will offer some material. Such tools can help uncover the keys to being a good communicator.

Prayer

Lord of all relationships, the hurts in marriage can be many and can leave deep wounds. I confess my own difficulties in this area and ask for the courage and wisdom to speak truth as I share my victories and failures in communicating with my husband.

Share Together

Believe it or not, conflicts about money, children, and even intimacy do not rank higher than poor communication for causing failure in marriage. Learning to express feelings, thoughts, and opinions is difficult. Knowing when to talk and where to share is also very important.

Acknowledge that there are differences in each relationship, accept the tools that work for all. Here are a few:

- Accept your husband.

- Respect your husband.

- Regard him as more important than yourself.

- Practice timing (when to say what).

- Offer humor. Laugh at yourself and help your mate to laugh at himself.

- Persevere. Remember, "The common begin, the uncommon finish."

Let's Talk About It

1. Do you sense that your husband keeps ideas, struggles, and joys from you?

2. Is conversation started but sometimes not finished? Do you know why?

3. Are you afraid to bring up sensitive issues with your mate?

4. Can you tell the difference between communication that handles the business of your marriage and communication that promotes growth in your relationship?

5. Did your parents offer a good model in communication?

Pray for Each Other

This is a sensitive issue. Look for ways to affirm your daughter-of-the-heart. Help her see the things that are going well in her marriage. Concentrate on thanking God for His unfailing help.

Grow Together

Narrow the broad topic of communication to one or two specifics that need attention in the week to come.

How to Simply Submit

Plan, Prepare, and Pray

Point your young friend to any of the passages listed below for reading prior to your appointment: *Hebrews 13:17; Ephesians 5:21-33; Titus 2:3-5;* and *1 Corinthians 11:3,9.*

Read and meditate on the selected Scriptures. Consider consulting books or articles on the subject of submission. Key concepts include: obedience, service, yielding, being under authority, subordination, subjection. Some of these terms have military connotations, which add some force to our ideas of submission.

The way the concept of submission is viewed by our culture has changed over the years. Look for a newspaper or magazine article that gives an example of lack of submission to authority.

Prayer

Father, how am I at submitting? Do I have a servant's heart? For the sake of unity and peace, am I willing to lay down my own ideas and desires? Help me to be forthright and open with my daughter-of-the-heart as we discuss this loaded topic.

Share Together

Most women have struggled over "giving in" to their husbands and will not find it difficult to contribute to this discussion. Make it clear that dependence on God is essential to successfully "be under" someone else, especially when that person is wrong.

Let's Talk About It

1. What outside sources can help or hinder you from submitting?

2. Describe a time when you saw how being under someone's authority brought peace, unity, or protection.

3. Is your husband the only person you must submit to? If you are not married, should you ever submit to another person?

4. What does God's Word say on this topic? Find at least one applicable Scripture passage.

5. What is a woman's role in the marriage relationship?

Pray for Each Other

Identify at least one area where submission to your husband is particularly difficult and one area where submission to another authority is a struggle, such as obeying the speed limit. Give these areas to God and ask Him to develop in you the submissive spirit that will please Him.

Grow Together

Decide if you want to commit to a specific act between now and your next session. Examples: I will pray for the person I have difficulty submitting to; I will submit in one new way to my husband; I will memorize Ephesians 5:21.

Meeting 18
Intimacy

Plan, Prepare, and Pray

Because of the tenderness of this topic, be sure to select your time and place wisely, making sure the choice of location will provide privacy.

Read and meditate on *Song of Solomon; 1 Corinthians 7:3-5;* and *1 Peter 3:7.* Ed and Gaye Wheat's book on marriage (*Intended for Pleasure,* Revell Books) is an excellent additional resource. Key thoughts: God's plan for intimacy in marriage; emotional intimacy; physical intimacy; spiritual intimacy; practical ways to nurture intimacy with your mate.

Be open to discussing how American culture views sex, marriage, adultery, and fornication. If these topics are hard for you to talk about, tell your daughter-in-the-Lord and let her lead the discussion. A medical book may be of some help to this conversation.

Prayer

Father, may the sensitive nature of this topic not hinder our oneness and desire to learn what Your instructions are for married people.

Share Together

Introduce today's topic with some light chatter about girl relationships as teenagers, comparing your era to hers.

Intimacy between two people should be just that: intimate. However, for the sake of this session, encourage your younger friend to share on an appropriate level an evaluation of the intimacy in her marriage. Is her husband satisfied with the frequency? Is she understanding God's clear statement that we no longer have charge over our own bodies; rather, our mates have charge over us?

Marriage has many levels of acceptance. When we open our hearts to our husbands, then we allow them access to our emotions. Wedding vows are traditionally sealed with a kiss, which signifies the admittance to the physical level between a man and a woman. Help your friend see how the plan of marriage compares to Jesus' relationship to the church.

Let's Talk About It

1. Would spending more time with your mate help the intimate side of your relationship?

2. What are some actions that could promote intimacy with your mate?

3. Do you have any fears regarding this area of your marriage?

4. Do you have any history that would affect your marriage relationship? (If yes, do not feel this must be discussed in this session, but be certain to express this to God and anyone involved so that healing can take place.)

5. Do you have good verbal communication with your mate?

Pray for Each Other

Be careful not to betray any confidences shared during your prayer request time.

Grow Together

Pray with compassion. The serious impact of what goes on behind closed doors is dramatic. Both you and your daughter-of-the-heart need to be mindful of the potential pain involved in marriage and intimacy.

Diagnosing Your Children

Plan, Prepare, and Pray

Read and meditate on *1 Corinthians 10:31; 7:7; Proverbs 22:29; Romans 12:3-8; 1 Corinthians 12;* and *Proverbs 22:6.* Refer to the following materials if possible: *Two Sides of Love; The Treasure Tree;* and *Please Understand Me II* (see Supplemental Reading List at the back of the book). Consider additional material for this section. If you have access to these resources, this may be the time to complete a personality profile, temperament evaluation, or spiritual gifts inventory. Many churches have these tools available.

Prayer

Lord, let me honestly examine how I am using what You have given me. I thank You for the privilege of bringing glory to my King with the good gifts You have granted.

Share Together

Have you ever suffered from an ailment? Of course! We have experienced common colds and flu viruses, at the very least. When these illnesses attack, we know what to do: take aspirin, drink plenty of fluids, and rest.

But what if you suffer from recurring headaches? Those painful symptoms are persistent, and you may fail to find any relief until one day a doctor pronounces, "These headaches are caused by poor vision." You order the new glasses he prescribes, voila, the headaches are gone? But not until the proper diagnosis is achieved do you find a course of direction that leads to eventual relief.

Raising children is just like that. It is essential to find out who they are, how they are "bent" in terms of temperament, environment, spiritual gifts (for those who have chosen Jesus), interests, and natural talents. All of these factors will help you direct this precious gift from God. (I suggest you pick up a copy of Doug and Katie Fortune's book *Discovering Your Children's Gifts*.)

For example, if your child is naturally talkative, God may use him or her to preach or teach. You will want to encourage this child's language skills and temper excessive verbal communication so that this gift will be a blessing to others.

Get the picture? Help your daughter-of-the-heart evaluate the gifts, abilities, and personalities of her children— and perhaps even for herself and her mate!

Let's Talk About It

1. Did you ever ask yourself why your children are so different from one another? From yourself? Now that you know the reason, how will this knowledge assist you in nurturing the character and potential of each little personality?

2. Was this information a part of your growing up? If not, can you see how it might have helped you? Describe.

3. What do you believe your spiritual gifts are? Are you using them faithfully?

4. Give a short profile of each of your family members.

5. If you have recognized something new about anyone in your family, describe how this new diagnosis will help you deal with that family member.

Pray for Each Other

It does take time and energy to observe and listen to children in order to discover why they do some of the things they do. Ask God to help you dig deeper. You may need to rearrange your schedule for a time to make these important evaluations.

Grow Together

Perhaps today's session challenged you to take action. If so, take the time now to create a plan for that action.

Training the Will of Your Children

Plan, Prepare, and Pray

Encourage your friend to read *Deuteronomy 6:6-10* before you get together. Read and meditate on *Deuteronomy 6:6-10; Proverbs 22:6; Genesis 14:14;* and *Colossians 3:21.* For further study, refer to *What Is a Family?* by Edith Schaeffer. Think about how your mother trained you and how you trained your children. Research and meditate on the differences between training and teaching.

Clip relevant articles on child training from Christian magazines to give your younger partner.

Prayer

Lord, reveal to me any mistakes in child training that I have made but have not acknowledged or confessed. Show me if and to whom I need to make restitution, and give me the strength and courage to do so. Help me direct this young woman to You, the most true parent, for her instruction and training.

Share Together

Ask your daughter-of-the-heart to share her frustrations concerning her children. Prompt her with these questions if necessary: Do they go to bed easily? Do you have to repeat yourself more than once when giving directions? Do they keep their rooms clean? How much TV do they watch?

The Hebrew word for "train" literally means to "rub the gullet." The word refers to a primitive practice of opening an infant's throat by pouring a liquid such as blood or saliva into his or her throat and then rubbing the outside of the throat. This prompted the child to breathe and swallow.

Training is different from teaching. Because young children do not have the cognitive ability to reason, training is a necessary and important step in their growth. For a two-year-old to respond to your "no," you must first have trained him or her to do so without teaching the reason for saying no. That teaching will come later. A child who is trained early is almost always able to be trained by the voice of God when he or she becomes accountable.

Let's Talk About It

1. Do you believe there are limitations in training a child? Why?

2. What are your ideas about breaking a child's spirit versus training his or her will?

3. How did your parents train you?

4. Describe a way you show your children you respect them.

5. Read each of the following situations and determine if the parental response in each situation represents one or more of these: a) breaking the spirit; b) encouraging the spirit; c) negatively reinforcing the will; or d) shaping the will. Try to come to some consensus in each situation. Think of ways the parental response could be improved.

   - Four-year-old Jessie spills her milk at supper while reaching for the butter, after she has been told twice to ask for what she wants. You immediately say, "Now what did you have to do that for?" You get up and clean up the mess yourself.

- Five-year-old David yells, "No, I won't!" when you tell him to come back and take his water toys out of the bathtub. You respond, "Until you pick up those toys I won't let you play with Johnny."

- Your 15-year-old forgot to fold the laundry while watching a special TV program for three hours last night. You ask him to do it when he gets home from school tonight instead of doing it yourself.

- Your nine-year-old repeatedly fails to make her bed before leaving for school in the morning, despite your instruction and training. You are expecting guests, so you make the bed for her.

- Your three-year-old refuses to eat the dinner placed before him. After trying to entice him to eat his favorite foods, you send him to his room without dinner.

Pray for Each Other

Pray for any training God may need to do in your own lives. It is never too late to be changed in the presence of a holy God. Pray for all the children God has placed in your lives, including daughters- and sons-of-the-heart. Hold hands and ask your heavenly Father to make your eyes and minds clear to all the training He wants to accomplish in your lives. Ask God to bless your young friend as she seeks to train her children effectively and lovingly in the ways of God.

Grow Together

Help your young partner identify a specific area in which she needs to train or retrain her child. Determine one thing she can do to begin the process.

Meeting 21
Disciplining Your Children

Plan, Prepare, and Pray

Ask your young friend to be thinking about her children and how they respond to discipline. Read and meditate on *Ephesians 6:1-4.* The topic of discipline can be complicated and controversial, so be careful to stick to God's Word and your own experiences. Prepare your heart to share how disciplined you are personally. Also be ready to talk about how you disciplined your children.

While it is generally not a good idea to compare one child with another, it is helpful to have a means of measuring the growth of each child you are responsible to raise. Prior to this session, you might prepare a chart that will show areas of maturity children should achieve at certain ages and phases of life. For example:

Age 2-3	Pick up toys Put things back where they belong Brush teeth Pull covers off the bed
Age 4	Set the table Be responsible for feeding and grooming a pet Make simple sandwich or cold cereal breakfast Help with housework: vacuum, dust furniture
Age 5	Help with dinner preparation: tear lettuce, butter bread Make bed Scour sink Make phone calls

Age 6	Choose clothing Keep room in order Prepare school lunch Tie own shoes Help mom or dad with more complicated cleaning jobs
Age 7	Take phone messages Water lawn Carry in the groceries Do flat ironing (use hankies and napkins so the children can iron them!)
Age 8	Be responsible for personal hygiene Sew on a button or mend a tear Help with cooking: read recipes, learn cooking instructions Help with young children Polish silver Sweep walkways
Age 9-10	Do chores without reminders Have a pen pal Help with the grocery shopping Clean bedroom and bath (vacuum, dust, scrub tub and toilets) Learn more about money management
Age 11	Earn money: babysitting, mother's helper, yardwork Learn about banking Have a clothing allowance

Prayer

Father in heaven, do I obey You and please You? Make my heart more in tune to obedience and discipline more than ever before.

Share Together

When you honor someone, you show merited respect. We are told by God to honor our parents simply because God put them in that position. Some parents have not earned that honor by deed and word, but it is not actions that grant them honor. Rather it's the title of parent that God has bestowed.

It will be valuable to discuss how your young friend dealt with her own parents. This is a session that can assist both of you in the area of personal discipline.

Elisabeth Elliot said, "Anything less than instant obedience is disobedience." Two key issues to discuss are: How fast do your children respond to your directives. Do they obey fully? Partial obedience is not accepted by God (see 1 Samuel 15—Saul and Agag) and should not be accepted by a parent. This training should start early, but it is never too late to start expecting obedience from our children. Check out "reality discipline." According to Dr. Kevin Leman:

> We never tell parents to punish. We tell them to discipline, train, and teach their kids, but that doesn't mean that there might not be some kind of "pain" or consequence involved. That's how the kids learn what the real world is like and how it works. Reality Discipline gives the child a chance to make his own decisions and then live with the result of his mistakes and his failures or his good choices and his successes. (Taken from www.flcministries.org, based on interview about *Parent Talk*, by Randy Carlson and Kevin Leman, 1993.)

Remember, it is never too late to begin learning and increasing our own levels of obedience.

Let's Talk About It

1. Do you view the word "discipline" as the "D" word? Why?

2. Have you ever read any books or attended any seminars on the subject of disciplining your children? Describe.

3. Do you practice reality discipline?

4. Are you and your husband in agreement about how to raise and discipline your children? If not, what do you think is God's response to your lack of agreement?

5. Discuss the impact of inadequate discipline in the family on the community and world at large.

Pray for Each Other

It is easier for children to learn order and discipline from a mother who is orderly and disciplined. Pray that your daughter-in-the-Lord will want to lead the way by her willingness to honor God and her own parents. Pray for the courage to live a disciplined life of obedience to God.

Grow Together

Decide if you want to commit to a specific response to the topic of the week. For example, you may choose to memorize Ephesians 6:1-4.

Praying for Your Children

Plan, Prepare, and Pray

Suggest that your daughter-of-the-heart become familiar with the verses and material below in order to prepare her heart for this topic. Read and meditate on *Exodus 20:12; Deuteronomy 6:5-9; Psalm 78:5-7;* and *1 Samuel 1* and *2.* If you have any material on the topic of prayer or specific prayers for children, incorporate that information into this session. (Share the poem "Prayer for Our Children" by Amy Carmichael on page 213.) This will be an excellent time to acknowledge others who have prayed for you or your children and to remember the prayers you prayed as you raised your children. (Stormie Omartian's *The Power of a Praying Parent* is an excellent resource!)

This time is an appropriate opportunity to help your young friend set up a prayer notebook. Keep it simple: Notebook paper and three-ring binders are always available, inexpensive, and easy to use. Perhaps you could shop together for these items, or you might want to give them as a gift.

Prayer

Once again, Lord, I humble myself before You. Help me recall how I prayed on behalf of my children, how often I did so, and how You answered those prayers. Please use me to instill a determination in the heart of this young woman to be found faithful in praying for her children.

Share Together

Ask your friend a question or two about the role of prayer in her life, then transition into the topic of praying for her children.

The Bible tells us that we are all born sinners. As mothers, it is important for us to recognize the sinful condition of our children's hearts even at birth. As we acknowledge their lost condition, we begin to pray immediately for their future conversion. In addition to praying, we can teach and train by example, by life-giving truths in God's Word, and by the eternal impact on our lives of Christ's life, death on the cross for our resurrection, and ascension into heaven.

Biblical illustrations of the power of prayer to change hearts is plentiful. God has granted us the responsibility to train, protect, and pray for our children. When, how, or where we pray is not as important as our commitment to pray individually and regularly for each of our gifts from God.

Let's Talk About It

1. Is prayer a regular part of your life? If so, describe how you established the priority of prayer in your life. If not, describe your efforts and difficulties in this area.

2. Who was, or is, the single most influential person in your spiritual journey? Has that person prayed for you?

3. Reflect on an answer to prayer that occurred in the last six months.

4. Have you ever written your prayers? If not, are you willing to give it a try?

5. Do you pray with your children as well as for your children?

Pray for Each Other

Today, take the time to pray for your children. Be really specific and thorough. This discipline will serve your children well. Such a prayer time also enriches the relationship of those praying together.

Grow Together

For the coming week, make a commitment to pray for your children. Be prepared to chat about your prayer experience during the next session.

Prayer Ideas

1. Pray that your children will fear the Lord and serve Him: "You shall fear only the LORD your God; and you shall worship Him and swear by His name" (Deuteronomy 6:13 NASB).

2. Pray that your children will know Christ as Savior early in life: "O God, You are my God; I shall seek You earnestly; my soul thirsts for You, my flesh yearns for You, in a dry and weary land where there is no water" (Psalm 63:1 NASB).

3. Pray that your children will hate sin: "Hate evil, you who love the LORD, who preserves the souls of His godly ones; He delivers them from the hand of the wicked" (Psalm 97:10 NASB).

4. Pray that your children will be caught when they're guilty: "It is good for me that I was afflicted, that I may learn Your statutes" (Psalm 119:71 NASB).

5. Pray that your children will have a responsible attitude in all their interpersonal relationships: "Then this Daniel began distinguishing himself among the commissioners and satraps because he possessed an extraordinary spirit, and the

king planned to appoint him over the entire kingdom" (Daniel 6:3 NASB).

6. Pray that your children will respect those in authority over them: "Every person is to be in subjection to the governing authorities. For there is no authority except from God, and those which exist are established by God" (Romans 13:1 NASB).

7. Pray that your children will desire the right kind of friends and be protected from the wrong kind: "My son, if sinners entice you, do not consent....Do not walk in the way with them. Keep your feet from their path" (Proverbs 1:10,15 NASB).

8. Pray that your children will be kept from the wrong mate and saved for the right one: "Do not be bound together with unbelievers; for what partnership have righteousness and lawlessness, or what fellowship has light with darkness" (2 Corinthians 6:14 NASB).

9. Pray that your children and their prospective mates will be kept pure until marriage: "Flee immorality...Do you not know that your body is a temple of the Holy Spirit who is in you, whom you have from God, and that you are not your own? For you have been bought with a price: therefore glorify God in your body" (1 Corinthians 6:18-20 NASB).

10. Pray that your children will learn to submit totally to God and actively resist Satan in all circumstances: "Submit therefore to God. Resist the devil and he will flee from you" (James 4:7 NASB).

11. Pray that your children will be single-hearted, willing to be sold out to Jesus: "I urge you, brethren, by the mercies of God, to present your bodies a living and holy sacrifice, acceptable to God, which is your spiritual service of worship. And do not be conformed to this world, but be transformed by the

renewing of your mind, so that you may prove what the will of God is, that which is good and acceptable and perfect" (Romans 12:1,2 NASB).

12. Pray that your children will be hedged in so they cannot find their way to wrong people or wrong places, and that wrong people cannot find their way to your children: "Therefore, behold, I will hedge up her way with thorns, and I will build a wall against her so that she cannot find her paths. She will pursue her lovers, but she will not overtake them; and she will seek them, but will not find them" (Hosea 2:6,7 NASB).

13. Pray that your children will have quick, repentant hearts: "Be gracious to me, O God, according to Your lovingkindness; according to the greatness of Your compassion blot out my transgressions. Wash me thoroughly from my iniquity and cleanse me from my sin. For I know my transgressions, and my sin is ever before me" (Psalm 51:1-3 NASB).

14. Pray that your children will honor you and your husband so all will go well with them: "Children, obey your parents in the Lord, for this is right. Honor your father and mother (which is the first commandment with a promise), so that it may be well with you, and that you may live long on the earth" (Ephesians 6:1-3 NASB).

15. Pray that your children will be teachable and able to take correction: "All your sons will be taught of the LORD; and the well-being of your sons will be great" (Isaiah 54:13 NASB); "a wise son accepts his father's discipline, but a scoffer does not listen to rebuke" (Proverbs 13:1 NASB).

16. Pray that your children's lives will bear the fruit of the Spirit: "The fruit of the Spirit is love, joy, peace, patience, kindness, goodness, faithfulness, gentleness, self-control; against such things there is no law" (Galatians 5:22,23 NASB).

17. Pray that your children will live by the Spirit and not gratify their flesh: "Walk by the Spirit, and you will not carry out the desire of the flesh" (Galatians 5:16 NASB).

18. Pray that your children will trust in the Lord for direction in their lives, including their occupation: "Trust in the LORD with all your heart and do not lean on your own understanding. In all your ways acknowledge Him, and He will make your paths straight" (Proverbs 3:5,6 NASB).

∼ *Mentoring Moment* ∼

Prayer for Our Children

"Father, hear us, we are praying,
Hear the words our hearts are saying,
We are praying for our children.

Keep them from the power of evil,
From the secret hidden peril,
Father, hear us for our children.

From the whirlpool that would suck them,
From the treacherous quicksand pluck them,
Father, hear us for our children.
From the wordling's hollow gladness
From the sting of faithless sadness,
Father, Father, keep our children.

Through life's troubled waters, steer them,
Through life's bitter battles cheer them,
Father, Father be thou near them.

Read the language of our longing,
Read the wordless pleadings thronging
Holy Father for our children.

And whereever they may bide,
   lead them home at eventide."

—AMY CARMICHAEL

---

* Amy Carmichael, "Prayer for Our Children," used by permission
of Christian Literature Crusade, Fort Washington, PA 19034.

The Ministry of Motherhood

Plan, Prepare, and Pray

Read and meditate on **Psalm 127:1,3,5** and **Proverbs 31; 14:1**.

This session will go so fast that you may want to plan ahead and spend two meetings on this topic. Perhaps making a list of related topics of interest would help sharpen the focus. Your list might include: breastfeeding, demand versus scheduled feeding, spanking, children's books and toys, and education.

Prayer

From the works of Edith Schaeffer to Erma Bombeck, millions of words have been written about motherhood. Jesus, take my heart and mind and reshape them to look like Your mother's. Mary said to the angel, 'Let it be to me according to your word,' and the world was changed. May I be the kind of mother who wants God's will first.

Share Together

Children are a gift from God. He uses them to mold your character, just as He will use you to shape them. Sarah Edwards and her husband, Jonathan, had 1400 descendants. The list of accomplishments is notable. These descendants include a United States vice president, 13 college presidents, 65 professors, and 66 doctors. While these careers are extraordinary, the most important task you can do for your children is to lead them to Jesus Christ. Education, credentials, and experiences do not mean as much as one simple confession of sin and acknowledgment of the need for a Savior.

At the same time, there are the day-to-day challenges of raising kids. Discuss the topics you've listed and share your own experiences.

Let's Talk About It

1. In a few sentences, describe motherhood.

2. Name the top five challenges you face as a mother.

3. What is the most thrilling part of being a mother in your home?

4. What did your mother do that you would like to repeat? Not repeat?

Pray for Each Other

For most young women, the delight of being a mother is never-ending, and yet each day holds difficulties and decisions that they feel ill-equipped to handle. Make this time of prayer a time of celebrating motherhood and the fact that God trusts His children to our care. Dwell on what an honor it is to be called "mother." When the session is complete, you and your daughter-of-the-heart want to have God's perspective on this often overwhelming responsibility.

Grow Together

Decide if there is anything you want to ask this young woman to accomplish relating to the subject of being a minister to her children. It is not necessary to assign a task weekly, but from time to time it will help her stay on track.

Pray together over the implementation of her commitment. Talk to God about the issues that trouble you in your attempts to please Him in your mothering role. Rejoice over His gifts, His hand of protection, and His omniscience in your family life.

Meeting 24
Learning to Love Your Children

Plan, Prepare, and Pray

Read and meditate on *1 John 4:7,8,21; 1 Corinthians 13; Proverbs 17:5; Mark 1:40-42; Philippians 4:8; Isaiah 66:12; Proverbs 21:19;* and *Proverbs 15:15*. This abundant material covers the concept of love and can be applied to practical ways a mother can love her children.

Do you have any poems about children, any books that talk about the ways to love and cherish children? If so, spend a little time reviewing this material. When this session is over, both of you should have a deeper sense of how God would like His children to be loved.

Prayer

Dearest Lord Jesus, You are love. You demonstrate that love every day and every way in the lives of all You have created. Help me be a channel of Your love to this young woman in my life. Help us discover ways to offer love to our children.

Share Together

As you begin this session, talk briefly about what it was like grow up in your family, and ask your friend to share a bit about her childhood.

Keep your children in mind as you explore the following expressions of love, all of which can be found in Scripture:

Give the choice of love. Commit to love because it is right, not because it feels good.

Give the words of love. We all need regular verbal assurance; children need it the most.

Give the touch of love. Research has confirmed the human need for physical touch. The need to be held and cuddled is especially critical for babies.

Give the encouragement of love. Put courage into those little people by letting them know you are their best fan and cheerleader.

Give the comfort of love. In times of pain or sadness, provide love's healing comfort.

Give the laughter of love. Laughter sets a pleasant mood, a bright tone. Make merriment a daily dose of love in your home.

Give the discipline of love. Discipline establishes boundaries for children, making them feel safe and secure.

Let's Talk About It

1. Have you ever felt unloving toward your children? Describe why this feeling bothered you.

2. With which of the previous expressions of love do you struggle the most? Do you know why?

3. Do you expect or desire your children to love and honor you?

4. Can you think back to something you learned to love as a child? What was it? How did you learn to love it?

5. Together, make a short list of ways you love your children.

Pray for Each Other

Share about a time you felt loved as a child, then share about a time you felt rejected. Ask God to use those experiences to mold you into a loving person today and in the future.

Grow Together

Did something in this session inspire you to respond in a specific way? Perhaps you would like to write a love letter to one of your children. Or maybe you can commit to touch each of them at least once a day. Then do it!

∼ *Mentoring Moment* ∼

---

*Sing together "Jesus Loves the Little Children"
and "Jesus Love Me."*

The Ministry of Your Mansion

Plan, Prepare, and Pray

Be prepared to discuss "mansions" (homes) for this session. If you have been meeting in her mansion, maybe you should have this session at your mansion. Or borrow the mansion of someone you know who has a great bent toward hospitality. Be creative.

Read and meditate on *Matthew 12:34,35; Proverbs 17:1; 1 Peter 4:9,10;* and *John 14:2,3.* Collect some magazines like *House Beautiful* or *Victoria.* If you can secure a copy of *Open Heart, Open Home* by Karen Mains, scan it for inspiration.

This is a grand time to talk about comforts in the home and the concepts of quiet, peace, and preparation. You may want to review other sessions that deal with the home in terms of traditions, menus, and organization.

Prayer

Lord, I am grateful to You for my dwelling place. Whatever its size or location, I want my mansion to be a place of love and mercy. Please sensitize me to the effect my home has on those who live and visit there. Let me examine my level of investment as a servant to the people I love.

Share Together

Share photos you collected out of magazines and talk about how color, design, and texture can create certain feelings and effects.

A woman's mansion is most often a reflection of herself. Do the members of your family feel grace and mercy, love and acceptance in your home? Or do they sense misery, critical thinking, judgment, and aloofness? Your home ministry is intended to uplift and encourage the people who live there and the guests who visit.

Whether your visitor is dropping in for a cup of coffee, attending a dinner party, or staying for two weeks, prepare your heart for ministry. The hospitality you deliver is a direct result of your heart condition. Hospitality is not the act of fixing a meal; it is opening a door, offering a smile, and bringing comfort to one of God's creatures.

Reach out—offer mercy, not misery.

Let's Talk About It

1. Are you available to meet the needs of your family members?

2. List five ways you serve your family daily. With what attitude is that service given?

3. When a guest arrives, does it seem like an intrusion? If so, examine why you react this way.

4. What was the mood of the home in which you grew up?

5. Reflect on mansions you love to visit.

Pray for Each Other

This is an excellent time to admit that we cannot always be "Miss Mercy" and it is unrealistic to expect to serve with a consistent amount of zeal. Ask God to reveal how mercy looks in action. If your heart is bitter, submit it to the Healer for softening and reshaping.

Grow Together

Decide if you want to commit to any specific steps in an effort to bring a fresh ministry to your mansion.

Meeting 26
Being the Keeper of Your Home

Plan, Prepare, and Pray

Ask your friend to read the verses for this session and to evaluate her own home on the basis of clutter, cleanliness, and orderliness. Read and meditate on *Proverbs 31; Titus 2:3-5;* and *Philippians 3:13,14.* You may want to read my book *Get More Done in Less Time* and give or loan a copy to the daughter-of-your-heart. Be ready to discuss priorities, order, and practical housekeeping tips.

Prepare some visual aids, such as pot holders, laundry sorting bags, purse organization pouches, a daily planner, children's toy sorters, feather dusters, polishes and cleaners, and other time-saving tools.

Prayer

Lord, help me see the connection between Your orderly creation and our need to desire and culti- vate order in our lives. Let me be willing to admit to a messy closet or confused filing system as I lead the discussion. No matter how organized I am, help me see where I need more order.

Share Together

Ask your younger partner about her mother's style of house- keeping. How does your friend continue to be affected by it?

Talk about which of these names best characterizes you: Messy Maggie, Confused Carol, or Neat Nancy. Try to describe how your family would be affected by these traits. Be sensitive to the fact that we all keep our homes differently, and there is no one "right way." However, God's Word does indicate that we should maintain peace, keep records, provide order, and persevere. These are prerequisites for a healthy, peaceful home and can be applied even to mundane tasks such as the daily maintenance of kitchens, bathrooms, and bedrooms. And keeping accurate financial records is essential to being good stewards!

Let's Talk About It

1. Are you prepared to invite people to your home spontaneously? If not, why?

2. Have you ever looked in vain for something you knew you had?

3 Do you spend time going over the same paperwork more than once because what you need is in a pile somewhere?

4. Do you have more than one unfinished project from the past two years?

5. Do you feel burdened with too many things to accomplish?

6. Is it hard for you to say no?

Pray for Each Other

Ask God for the courage to submit one messy place in your home to Him. It may be a car full of junk, photos that need to be mounted into albums, a catch-all drawer in the kitchen, or the top shelf of your closet. Seek joy from the Lord in the process of bringing order from chaos.

Grow Together

Decide if you want to commit to cleaning up the area you prayed about. Pray together. Let the frustrations of undone work spill out of your hearts. Acknowledge that you can put past failures behind and move ahead to apply principles of order.

∼ *Mentoring Moment* ∼

"It is not what you do that makes you tired,
but what you don't do."

Meeting 27
Food, Menus, and Hospitality

Plan, Prepare, and Pray

Clear enough time on your schedule to do this session as a project, if possible. Invite your young friend to join you in planning a menu, making a shopping list, and doing the marketing. This will be fun for both of you.

Read and meditate on **Proverbs 31; Titus 2:3-5; 1 Peter 4:9;** and **Romans 12:13**. If you have the book, read chapters 5 and 14 of *Get More Done in Less Time*.

Prepare a menu plan for one week as an example to share with your daughter-of-the-heart. Give this menu plan to her at the conclusion of your time together. Pull out a few of your favorite recipes, making sure that some are easy. It might also be fun to introduce your young friend to favorite kitchen tools and tell her why you find them so useful.

Prayer

Father, You ask us to redeem our time and be good stewards of our money. May this extremely practical session help us honor You.

Share Together

Start your conversation by talking about houseguests, having company for dinner, and throwing parties. Share your greatest defeat and your greatest victory in these categories!

Together, prepare a complete menu plan, for your young friend's week. As you make the plan, create a grocery list of the items you will need to prepare each of these meals. Then, when you get to the market, make sure your head is not turned by a pretty bunch of asparagus—unless asparagus is on your list!

The topic of hospitality is very important to the heart of God. As His people, we are His hands. Hospitality starts with hands that hold doors open for others in public places, pat small children with affection, and touch someone's shoulder or arm when a moment of comfort is needed. These same hands maintain an orderly home and prepare meals to serve daily to families and guests.

The art of hospitality must not be lost. Encourage this younger woman to open her doors often to anyone God may send. We should not wait for the "right time" or the "right stuff." If we do, we may lose a blessing.

Let's Talk About It

1. Did you grow up in a home that welcomed people or one that made them feel uncomfortable?

2. Do you feel it is just too much work to prepare for extra guests in your home?

3. What do you think Scripture means when it tells us to practice hospitality without grumbling and complaining? What do you usually do?

4. What is your biggest fear about having guests for dinner? What can you actively do about this concern?

5. If you have planned menus in the past, why did you stop?

6. Discuss a party that you went to that made you smile. What ingredients did the event offer?

Pray for Each Other

For us older women it is easy to put aside regular meal preparation and the habit of opening our homes to others. After all, we did our part already, right? For young women it is easy to believe there will be many other opportunities and that they should wait until the dishes match. Ask God to give both of you the energy and desire to share all that belongs to Him with others.

Grow Together

Decide to complete one more menu plan before you meet again. Make a general chart outline and photocopy it so you can continue to plan! Pray together. This practical information on hospitality has a way of changing our focus. As we become more efficient, we have more energy and time for others.

∼ *Mentoring Moment* ∼

Broccoli Chowder
by Donna Otto
(I serve this chowder every Thanksgiving.)

Ingredients

2 pounds fresh broccoli	2 tsp. salt
3 12 ½ oz. cans chicken broth	2 cups milk
¼ tsp. pepper (white preferred)	1 cup light cream
½ pound Swiss cheese, grated	¼ cup butter
1 cup chopped, cooked (shaved)ham	

Instruction

In a large covered kettle cook broccoli in one can of chicken broth for about seven minutes, or until tender. Remove broccoli from broth, cool and chop coarsely. Add remaining chicken broth, milk, ham, salt, and pepper. Bring to boil over medium heat, stirring occasionally. Stir in remaining ingredients, adding light cream last. Be sure not to boil after cream is added as it will curdle.

Menu Planner   Date:

	Breakfast	Lunch	Dinner
S U N			
M O N			
T U E S			
W E D			
T H U R			
F R I			
S A T			

Meeting 28
Finances and Budgets

Plan, Prepare, and Pray

Read and meditate on *Philippians 4:11,12; Matthew 5:14; 25:15-30; 1 Timothy 6:18;* and *Matthew 25:24-30.* Any material you have in your resources by Larry Burkett or Ron Blue, both excellent money managers who write on the topic from a Christian perspective, will be helpful. If you do not manage the household budget in your family, talk to a few people who do handle the budgeting, purchasing, and bill-paying in their homes. Reflect on your own spending and saving practices.

If you use a budgeting system, be prepared to share it during your time together. If not, you will be able to find a sample budget worksheet in any of Burkett's or Blue's books.

Prayer

> *Lord, help me to see and understand the different sides of this issue. Is money for spending or saving? Is there a balance presented in Your Word that will provide an answer? Am I a good steward, as described in Matthew 25?*

Share Together

Get a feel for the way your young friend handles her finances. Remember that money is a personal topic to discuss with anyone, so be sensitive.

This is a truly perfect time to talk about priorities. It is important to establish how we consume our two great tangible resources: possessions and money. The heart of the issue regarding money is stewardship. We all need to understand that we own nothing. What we have is a gift from God, and He can do whatever He desires with His possessions. Our responsibility as stewards is to use all He has entrusted to us to bring glory to Him. This concept seems simple, but it can be difficult to accomplish.

As stewards, we are tasked with saving, investing, giving, and spending. Try to help your friend discover for herself if she handles each of these areas equally well. If not, which one does she have the most difficulty with? Suggest how her early training experiences may have contributed to her attitude toward finances. Also, present the format for establishing a budget if her family does not already use one. Be careful not to intrude on the husband/wife decision-making in this area.

Let's Talk About It

1. How did your parents handle money? Were they in agreement?

2. At what age were you given a degree of responsibility to handle money?

3. In terms of finances, do you think God is disappointed with you in any area? If so, which one?

4. Do you and your husband agree on money matters? If not, what stands in the way of your agreement? Can you effect change?

5. Is there a maximum amount of money you can spend without consulting your husband? If finances are tight, you may find it helpful to establish a specific dollar amount as a ceiling of individual spending in your household.

Pray for Each Other

Ask the Lord for honesty as you consider whether you tend to buy things in an attempt to satisfy another needy area in your life. Ask Jesus to replace any faulty financial philosophy with biblical thinking.

Grow Together

Decide if you want to commit to any specific change in the area of finances. For example, before making a purchase you could ask yourself, "Do I really need this or do I just want it?" Pray together. The needs we try to meet with money are enormous. Take time to ask God to help you be wise and careful with the resources He has given you permission to use.

Meeting 29
Feathering Your Nest

Plan, Prepare, and Pray

Read and meditate on *Proverbs 31*. This session presents an opportunity for the two of you to have fun "talking house." Share about the time you painted your bedroom a lovely shade of soft pink that dried "hot pink." Commiserate about putting up with the wrong color of carpet until it wears out. Remember a time when God asked you to wait for what you wanted and another time when God let you go first class.

Head for the library or magazine stand to find home decorating publications with inspiring pictures and tips for decorating on a budget. Find practical articles on such subjects as how to cover ceramic tile without buying new tile. If you have a friend in the interior design business, borrow some fabric books and consult her expertise for ideas to share with your young friend. Keep in mind your daughter-in-the-Lord may know more than you do about design. Give her a chance to shine!

Prayer

Lord, help me to effectively communicate Your perspective on our earthly dwellings. May we learn to 'feather our nests' without overdoing it.

Share Together

Ask your young woman to recall the houses or apartments she grew up in. Find out if they were city or country dwellings. Get a feel for which she prefers.

Rely on your resources to give you design ideas for discussion, and then draw on your relationship as you talk about what makes a house a home. Building a warm, welcoming atmosphere takes heart and love and a hand of grace—not necessarily a generous budget. Paint covers anything as easily (and more cheaply) as fabulous wallpapers can. Invite your friend to consider whether she has done all she can with her resources. Does her nest creatively express who she is and what she wants her family and friends to feel?

Let's Talk About It

1. How do you feel you could better manage your home? This is an excellent time to refer to related sessions that address organization, budgeting, and financial management.

2. Do you like having guests in your home? Are you comfortable feeding them whatever you can rustle up?

3. Do people often tell you how welcome they feel in your home? If not, can you explain why not?

4. Have you ever transformed a room from ugly to beautiful? If so, take time to share the experience.

5. Are there little things you know that could be done right now to "feather up" your nest? Each of you make a list, then share them.

Pray for Each Other

Share with the Lord your desires and frustrations about creating a pleasant home environment. Ask the Creator of all things to bring ideas and resources into your mind that will fit into your time and money budget.

Grow Together

The two of you might like to tackle a project together. Perhaps you both have silk flower arrangements that need to be refreshed or furniture that could be arranged to better advantage. Set a time when you can help each other accomplish the task you select. Pray together. Rejoice in the common womanly challenge of trying to make a house a home. If money is no object, remember that it is possible to buy lots of stuff and still fail to make people comfortable in your environment. If there is little money to spare, it is easy to forget that even a small piece of bright fabric will dress up a table and set a cheerful mood for your next family meal.

Meeting 30
Creating Family Memories

Plan, Prepare, and Pray

Ask your younger partner to come prepared to talk about meaningful traditions in her family.

Read and meditate on *Psalm 22:2; 112:6; Isaiah 49:15; Luke 12:11,12;* and *Hebrews 2:1.* Look for other material that highlights creating memories for the purpose of recording and recalling special events. Think about some memories you have created for others and those you treasure for yourself.

You need time and perseverance in the face of obstacles when you attempt to create memories. Consider the effort it takes to prepare for a surprise party, wedding, or other major event. At the same time, remember that the small traditions of the home are equally important.

Prayer

Lord, I want to remember You first and foremost. Help me create memories that strengthen my family and honor you.

Share Together

Ask your dear daughter-of-the-heart about her memories of childhood, school days, and courtship. Point out that there is usually a key person responsible for planning a memory we cherish.

Each of us can give the gift of creating a memory. It can be as simple as piling sugar and cinnamon on toast every Saturday or as complicated as a surprise party with 400 guests. Holidays are times to establish traditions: a favorite vegetable dish that is only made at Thanksgiving, the huge candle that shows up on everyone's birthday cake, or the Easter basket that reappears every year with the family's favorite treats. Love is what makes the event. Perseverance may be required to push past the reserve of husband or the embarrassment of your teenager. Be willing to run the risk of rejection—it's worth it!

Your discussion of the special memories created by others will hopefully inspire this young woman to want to do the same for the people God has placed in her world.

Let's Talk About It

1. Have you been hesitant to try to create a memory for someone who has rejected your attempts in the past?

2. Are you willing to risk rejection to create a memory that might bring a smile to someone's heart?

3. What would keep you from exerting the energy necessary to create a memory?

4. Have you ever wished that the family you grew up in had more traditions? Explain. Does this make you want to create memories for your loved ones, or does it make you afraid to try?

Pray for Each Other

During this session, you can talk about the traditions and memories found in the Scriptures. What traditions did Jesus start?

Grow Together

The two of you might enjoy planning a memory-making event together. Consult your calendars. Is there a holiday coming soon that would be useful as a starting point to plan a new tradition in your families? If not, make up a reason and plan away!

Mentors for Mothers

Answering the Call to Become a Mentor

~

"Please sing it again, Grandma Sybil!" the little boy said into the telephone. And gladly she did:

> *Two little eyes to look to God*
> *Two little ears to hear His Word*
> *Two little feet to walk His ways*
> *Two little lips to sing His praise*
> *Two little hands to do His will*
> *And one little heart to love Him still.*

"Grandma Sybil" is an honorary title. Despite the obvious mutual affection, she's not related to this little boy by blood. Instead, she is an older woman of God who has taken seriously His command in Titus 2 and responded by joining Mentor for Mothers, a program I founded 12 years ago. She is now a mentor for a young mom who has truly become a daughter of the heart.

Now, mentors in my program aren't required to know the words to children's songs (and the hand gestures that go along), but they are required to know the Word of God. Most of our mentors know both! Grandma Sybil knows the right kind of songs for her daughter of the heart's young son, and she also knows the Word of God and what it has for daughters-of-the-heart today. Mentors for Mothers brings older women like Sybil together with younger moms in a Titus 2 relationship. Let me tell you more about the program.

Mentors for Mothers: An Overview

Since all my life I have been so strongly and so positively influenced by the older women God has placed along my path, I deeply desired to find a way to help other young women experience the rich blessings of such relationships. My home church—Scottsdale Bible Church in Arizona—seemed the best place to start. So in 1991, Joan Malouf and I put our heads together, drafted a proposal, consulted with our church staff, and began Mentors for Mothers. (We're pleased that the program—whose title was quickly shortened to "M4Ms" and whose trademark instantly became snacking on M&Ms—now has a permanent place in the courses offered the women of our church each year.)

The purpose of the program? To give young women the opportunity to hear and be encouraged by an older woman's godly perspective on life. And, defined from the other side, to give older women the opportunity to respond to God's call to ministry in Titus 2. By now, you know the mandate:

> Older women likewise are to be reverent in their behavior, not malicious gossips, not enslaved to much wine, teaching what is good, that they may encourage the young women to love their husbands, to love their children, to be sensible, pure, workers at home, kind, being subject to their own husbands, that the Word of God may not be dishonored (Titus 2:3-5).

The lead M4M teacher presents the material to an audience of twosomes, each comprised of an older woman and a young mother. These pairs offer each other the accountability, sharing, authenticity, confidentiality, and prayer support found in a typical church small group. As some of the letters found in chapter 9 reflect, the program has been well accepted, and women of all ages have benefited greatly.

The Role of Prayer

One of the significant elements in this God-ordained relationship between a younger woman and an older woman is the older woman's faithful prayers for her mom. No one can know the vital role such prayer plays in the older woman's ministry and the younger woman's struggles.

Praying for her young woman's walk with the Lord, her need for His protection, and her ability to hear His voice keeps the mentor mindful of her major goals and the bigger issues of a young woman's life. Of course the older woman also prays about the specific and daily concerns her young mother talks about. And then there are those issues which are somewhat unique to the 21st century...

The Needs in the 21st Century

One day, I met a 30-year-old woman, an attorney with one child. She and her husband had just moved to Scottsdale from Oklahoma when she met a woman at a park who said, "Oh, yes! I'm a stay-at-home mom and I love it. Come hear our teacher."

After her first class with Mentors for Mothers, this young woman came to me and said, "I'm thirty years old and I've never heard anyone tell me to stay at home. Not a single person!" Her parents, her education, her circle of friends, and certainly her work environment all said,

"Work!" But she decided to ignore those voices. She became an active part of this young mothers' group and chose to stay at home and have another child. What fun to watch her grow as she felt encouraged and supported to do what God had told her!

And she's not the only mom who has found the support she needed in Mentors for Mothers. I recently received a letter from a brand-new mom who said, "I am feeling a great deal of pressure to put my baby in the mom's morning out program or to at least give her a bottle instead of breastfeeding her so I can get some relief. Donna, I need help. I love being home, and I want my little girl to sleep in her own bed when she naps, not the car seat because her mom is running around. Please give me some assistance."

How I wish all my letters were so easy to respond to! I told her, without hesitation, "Yes, yes! A thousand times yes! Stay at home and care for your loved ones. You will never be sorry!" She knew what her heart was telling her to do. All she needed was affirmation—or, to use a more current word, validation—for her choice. And older women like you and me—women who have raised their children—can offer that much-needed support to today's younger generation. These women are the most educated who have ever walked on the planet (most of them have a four-year college degree and some have postgraduate work), but they need you, the older woman, to affirm their difficult choice to stay at home with their children.

From what I see, women in the 21st century also struggle with the closely related issues of commitment and responsibility. The young wife or mother who was raised in a broken home may struggle with what commitment looks like—"Can I make a commitment and keep it? Will my husband make commitments and keep them? How can I teach our children about commitment?" Responsibility is the ability to follow through on a commitment. It's saying "yes" to a project and then seeing it through to completion even when the task gets more difficult than anticipated.

What evidence do I have that people of the 21st century don't understand responsibility and commitment? Consider that the simple act of responding to an invitation's RSVP is a dying art. These days, parents of the bride are aghast at the poor response to formal wedding invitations. Even more troublesome are the individuals who responsibly call and say "yes" but then do not attend! They don't follow through on their commitment; they don't complete the task. Trained differently than the 21st century woman was, the older woman understands commitment and responsibility, she knows the importance of fulfilling obligations, and she can pass this knowledge on to a young wife and mom. Commitment and responsibility, simple courtesy and basic good manners—these are simple but important gifts that older women can pass on to their younger counterparts. And that's some of what happens in Mentors for Mothers.

Other Lessons for Life

During the years that I've watched older and younger women come together in Mentors for Mothers, I've also seen young moms benefit from lessons older women have learned about the pain and suffering that life brings. I know that, a few years ago, when we moved my 87-year-old father-in-law into our home, I looked for a woman who had already walked through the last years of her parents' lives. subscribed to *Parent Advisor* and read articles on caring for the aged and the children's role in a parent's life. But what helped most were the words of women who had lived through what I was now experiencing, who had watched a physically strong man undergo the attacks of Alzheimer's disease and be left sadly confused, who knew the whole gamut of emotions—uprootedness, helplessness, frustration, sadness—that I was feeling.

As I think back on that time when Poppa was in our home, I must also mention the invaluable help I received from two daughters of my heart during this difficult season. Cliffy came to our home for a month, and five days a week she was available to help me. Jen also came alongside to do for me what I couldn't do for myself at that time. I will always be grateful to these dear young women who were by my side lightening the load when the days were long and hard.

Whether we're young or old, it's easier to deal with life's hard times when we don't go it alone—and that's what a Titus 2 ministry is all about. An older woman can keep a younger woman from having to go it alone by being there with her. The older woman can also offer reassurance that she's a kindred spirit, that she knows pain, and, often, that she's experienced the same circumstances. A difficult pregnancy, a miscarriage, the death of a child, financial struggles, a job loss, a family crisis, marital problems—these things and more bring us pain. And when pain comes to a younger woman, an older woman can be available, willing to listen, and willing to walk alongside her. She can also, when the moment is right, offer the perspective that God uses life's hard times to draw us close to Him, refine our faith, and make us more like Christ. I've found that, if an older woman is one who blesses, she is one who has experienced the hardest of life and has learned the value of trials and joy in the midst of them. She has clung to the words of 1 Peter 1:6,7 ("In this you greatly rejoice, even though now for a little while, if necessary, you have been distressed by various trials, that the proof of your faith, being more precious than gold which is perishable, even though tested by fire, may be found to result in praise and glory and honor at the revelation of Jesus Christ"), and now she can offer that same hope to the younger woman who is hurting.

Passing on this wisdom, sharing her love of God, and testifying to His faithfulness and goodness is what an older woman is called to do. God commands us to pass on His ways to the next generation. When the Navajo people neglected that duty, American cowboy artist Ray Swanson stepped in and, through his painting, preserved art forms of the Navajo culture. He is an example to us as we share the art and culture of becoming godly women, building a marriage that glorifies God, caring for our children as God would have us do, and making our home a peaceful place that welcomes people in the Lord's name. This entails much that is mundane (ironing shirts, setting the table, preparing meals, changing diapers, scrubbing toilets—you know the list!), but even in that an older woman can help and be a beacon of God's light when she does. After all, how often, when you were a young homemaker, did you struggle with a recipe only to have an older, more experienced woman say, "Here! Try this! It's easy and delicious!" We older women can do the same thing for our younger woman's life outside the kitchen—for her spiritual life, her marriage, her mothering, and her homemaking. Indeed, what a privilege!

That I Can Do!

Marie Peterson, wife of composer/musician John W. Peterson and a fellow church member, has always kept a low profile. By choice, she has stayed out of the limelight. Through the years, I've occasionally asked her to sit on a panel or let me interview her. I'd receive a polite but firm "no" after which she would often add, "I don't have anything to say. I've always been John's wife and the girls' mother—nothing more, nothing less." Despite the fact that those tasks are incredibly important and she did an above average job, Marie did not feel called to speak publicly.

Well, when Mentors for Mothers began, I went to her again and asked her to be involved. This time her response was a hearty "Yes! That I can do!"—and she did a wonderful job. The fortunate young mother who had Marie as her older woman will be blessed all her life by Marie's godly and rich perspective on living in a way that glorifies God.

So you don't fancy yourself a Marie? Then think of Grandma Sybil. Remember her little song? Even if that's all she'd had to give, I'm confident that—as she said, "Here I am" in obedience to God and as she entered into this special Titus 2 relationship—she would have trusted Him that it was enough to give. So if you feel you don't have much to give, I say to you, "Trust God, as many older women before you have, that what He's given you—even if it's 'just' a children's song and a desire to obey Him—is enough for you to do the ministry He's called you to." When God calls, He empowers and in that little book of Titus He's clearly calling you to pass on to the next gener ation your love for Him and your knowledge of His ways.

Supplemental Reading List

~

Doug and Katie Fortune, *Discover Your Children's Gifts* (Chosen Books).

Bill Hybels, *Fit to be Tied* (book published by Zondervan, audiotape distributed by Willow Creek Community Church, Barrington, Illinois).

Donna Otto, *Get More Done in Less Time* (Harvest House).

Willard F. Harley Jr., *His Needs, Her Needs* (Revell).

Gary Smalley and John Trent, *The Language of Love* (Pocket Books).

Gloria Gaither and Shirley Dobson, *Let's Make a Memory* (Word).

Larry Crabb, *The Marriage Builder* (Zondervan).

Ron Blue, *Master Your Money* (Thomas Nelson).

Karen Mains, *Open Heart, Open Home* (Mainstay Church Resources).

David Kiersey, *Please Understand Me II* (Prometheus Nemesis Book Company).

Stormie Omartian, *The Power of a Praying Parent* (Harvest House).

Stormie Omartian, *The Power of a Praying Wife* (Harvest House).

Donna Otto, *Stay at Home Mom* (Harvest House Publishers).

Gary Smalley and John Trent, *Two Sides of Love* (Focus on the Family).

Doris Greig, *We Didn't Know They Were Angels* (Regal Books).

John Trent, *The Treasure Tree* (Word).

Edith Schaeffer, *What Is a Family?* (Baker Book House).

Additional Recommendations

Elisabeth Elliot, *Discipline: The Glad Surrender* (Revell).

H. Clay Trumbell, *Hints on Child Training* (Great Expectations Book Company).

Elizabeth Rice Handford, *Me? Obey Him?* (Sword of the Lord).

Elisabeth Elliot, *The Shaping of a Christian Family* (Revell).

Emilie Barnes, *Spirit of Loveliness*

Emilie Barnes and Donna Otto, *Friends of the Heart*

For more information on
Donna Otto's ministry or if
you would like her
to address your group, contact:
Donna Otto
11453 North 53rd Place
Scottsdale, AZ 85254
480-991-7464

Other Books by Donna Otto

Secrets to Getting More Done in Less Time (MARCH 2006)

Providing easy-to-follow ideas, practical charts, and specific suggestions for many areas of life management, Donna helps you maximize your day so you have more time for the fun stuff! Discover ways to save thousands of steps in the kitchen, streamline your shopping, create joyful holiday gatherings, make your daily planner work for you, and more! If you want to have more energy, feel better physically and mentally, and decrease your frustration, *Get More Done in Less Time* will help you.

The Stay-at-Home Mom

Whether you're a career woman considering staying at home or a full-time homemaker, you'll appreciate Donna's wealth of insight and information. Applauding and cheering on moms who stay home with their children, she offers practical ideas to make the journey a fulfilling, successful adventure in areas that include finance, organization, children's education choices, and goal-setting. With boundless enthusiasm for home and personal organization, she presents the challenges and joys of being a stay-at-home mom.

Finding Your Purpose as a Mom

Helping women share the joys and pains of everyday life, mentoring provides a venue for discussing effective strategies for navigating the demands of being a wife, mother, friend, and businesswoman. Mentoring helps women—

- Understand God's unique purpose for their lives
- Makes better use of time, skills, and spiritual gifts
- Cultivates a stronger faith and trust in God

Donna shows how to develop and nourish a mentoring relationship that will produce abundant spiritual fruit. (Condensed from *Between Women of God* and *The Gentle Art of Mentoring*.)